INVESTED

INVESTED

The New Science, Strategy, & System of Used Vehicle Investment Management

DALE POLLAK
WITH LANCE HELGESON

GREENLEAF
BOOK GROUP PRESS

Published by vAuto Press
Oakbrook Terrace, IL
www.vauto.com

Distributed by Greenleaf Book Group

For ordering information or special discounts for bulk purchases, please contact Greenleaf Book Group at PO Box 91869, Austin, TX 78709, 512.891.6100.

Design and composition by Greenleaf Book Group
Cover design by Greenleaf Book Group

Publisher's Cataloging-in-Publication data is available.

Print ISBN: 979-8-9857690-1-2

eBook ISBN: 979-8-9857690-3-6

To offset the number of trees consumed in the printing of our books, Greenleaf donates a portion of the proceeds from each printing to the Arbor Day Foundation. Greenleaf Book Group has replaced over 50,000 trees since 2007.

Printed in the United States of America on acid-free paper

22 23 24 25 26 27 10 9 8 7 6 5 4 3 2 1

First Edition

CONTENTS

PREFACE

LOOKING BACK AND FORWARD

As I pen this preface, I find myself reflecting on the winding journey that has been my career in the retail automotive industry.

The title of this book, *Invested*, carries a dual significance that resonates deeply with me. On one hand, it speaks to a new era of investment management strategy, specifically tailored to used vehicle operations, a field that has been both my passion and my pursuit. On the other hand, it reflects the personal investment I have made during my career to help dealers.

When I first set foot in this industry, I was driven by a desire to innovate, to create solutions that would not only streamline operations but also transform how we perceive value and success for used vehicle departments. The years that followed were marked by challenges, triumphs, and an unwavering commitment to excellence.

Each innovation, each step forward was an investment in a vision I believed could redefine our industry.

Now, as I anticipate the future, I am filled with excitement and curiosity. As I think about what's to come, it brings a profound contemplation of what it means to invest a lifetime into something greater than oneself. While I have witnessed the tangible returns of my efforts in the form of appreciation and the respect of the industry and the people I have had the privilege to serve, there is a lingering question: How will I continue to realize the investment return from my work as I have in the past?

But right now, all that matters is the imperative for dealers to better understand what has already arrived—another critical moment of redefinition for our industry.

Invested is not just a manual for managing used car operations; it is a testament to the enduring principles of investment, both financial and personal. It is an exploration of how strategic thinking and innovative management can yield significant returns, not only in profit but in the legacy one leaves behind.

As you delve into the pages that follow, I hope you find not only practical wisdom but also an invitation to reflect on your own investments. May this work inspire you to pursue excellence with the same fervor and dedication that has driven me throughout my career.

And may you discover, as I have, that the true measure of investment is not solely in the returns we can quantify, but in the lasting impact on our industry and the people we serve.

In gratitude and anticipation,
—Dale

INTRODUCTION

THE CASE FOR USED VEHICLE INVESTMENT MANAGEMENT STRATEGY

If you asked a used vehicle manager why they come to work every day, they'd most likely tell you it's to "sell cars."

This understanding of a manager's primary responsibility is closely tied to how many dealers and managers regard themselves: I'm a "car guy," a "car gal," or a "car person."

There's nothing inherently wrong with this identity. After all, a primary function of the used vehicle department is, in fact, to sell cars.

But I would submit that selling cars isn't the *primary* reason we show up to work every day. I would also submit that much of the distress and trouble that manifests in used vehicle departments across the country today owes to the lack of understanding of what our true purpose should be. It makes me wonder if we've all been wrong for decades, at least on some level, about how we manage our used vehicle operations.

No one can argue with this important fact: Our primary purpose for acquiring, pricing, and managing used vehicles is to make a net profit for the used vehicle department and the dealership. To do this, we invest money in assets or merchandise, which just happen to be used vehicles, for the purpose of making a return on the investment.

That's why I don't think it's exactly correct for us to believe we are, and regard ourselves as, just "car people." In fact, this view diminishes the importance of the used vehicle department, and the roles and responsibilities of the people who manage it. As many dealers know, the used vehicle department is the only engine inside a dealership that drives revenue and gross profit across every department. You could make the case that as the net profit in the used vehicle department goes, so goes the net profit for the entire dealership.

Instead of thinking of ourselves as car people, I think we'd be far better off, as individuals with used vehicle department oversight and responsibility, and as an industry, to consider ourselves money managers. Furthermore, we should strive to believe and behave as prudent managers of money. We should embrace the fact that our primary purpose and reason for coming to work is to optimize the investment return of every used vehicle investment for the purpose of delivering a positive net profit.

But as we explore in this book, our identity as car people, as managers of merchandise, is deeply entrenched and difficult to undo. Even so, I believe it's now imperative that dealers and their used vehicle managers make this transition sooner rather than later.

I say this because the post-pandemic market for used vehicles is far more challenging than anything we've seen in the past. The retail and wholesale markets for used vehicles are far more efficient than they used to be. Neither market operates in a singular fashion. Rather, each has its own pockets of opportunity and risk in ways that didn't manifest, or perhaps we were unaware of, than in the past.

It's also true that, as an industry, we currently possess very little, if any, investment management acumen and aptitude when it comes to properly managing the money invested in used vehicles to drive optimal investment returns and net profit. You don't have to look too far to find evidence of this deficiency.

For example, if I asked any good car person how many used vehicles they sold in the last month, they'd know the answer off the top of their head. Same for their average front-end gross. But if I asked them to tell me the net profit their used vehicle department generated in a prior month, they wouldn't be able to answer the question without looking it up. Isn't that a bit strange? If our primary purpose in used vehicles is to deliver a net profit for the department and dealership, shouldn't we be as dialed into this figure as much, if not more so, than the other important departmental metrics?

Unfortunately, that's not the current case. The net profit number, which represents the primary reason we come to work, is the least familiar to us.

Here's another example that involves three different investment scenarios:

1. You invested $20,000 in a vehicle, sold it in seven days, and made a $1,000 gross profit.

2. You invested $20,000 in a vehicle, sold it in 45 days, and made a $1,800 gross profit.

3. You invested $20,000 in a vehicle, sold it in 60 days, and made a $3,000 gross profit.

I suspect a first-year investment management student would know the answer to the question of which scenario would represent the highest return on investment. But when I pose these scenarios to good used car people, they have no idea what the correct answer might be. If I pushed them, they'd probably think the $3,000 gross profit is the best outcome.

But in fact, the vehicle that sold in seven days and generated a $1,000 gross profit yields the best annualized return on investment, at 177 percent. The second-best outcome is the vehicle that sold in 60 days and generated a 101 percent annualized return. The worst investment of the three is the vehicle that generated $1,800 gross after 45 days, which amounts to a 73 percent annualized return.

Think about that. Not one of us would know the answer. How odd is that? How weird is it, especially when our primary purpose in used vehicles is to optimize investment returns in the interest of delivering a net profit for the department, that we can't readily identify the investment outcome that delivers the best return in those three scenarios?

Let's take yet another example. If you were a money manager and you had two identical used vehicle investments—same make, year, model, condition, and mileage—it would be completely appropriate to price those vehicles differently. But a car person wouldn't think that way. It'd be weird, even wrong, to price them differently. How could you do that when they're exactly the same car?

That's perfectly reasonable thinking if you're a car person who's focused on managing cars and merchandise. There'd be no justification for pricing one vehicle differently than the other. They are the same car. But that's not what a prudent investment or money manager would do. They'd price them differently. Why? Well, what if you owned one vehicle for 98 percent Cost to Market and the other for 85 percent Cost to Market? If it was your money invested in those vehicles, wouldn't you have a vested interest in selling one faster than the other?

The answer is, yes, of course. But that's not how we, as car people, think. That's not a principle in the traditional used vehicle playbook, because everything we've been taught to think or do revolves around our roles as car people, who manage vehicles and merchandise, not investments.

Therein lies a critical question we, as car people, must consider: Have we been wrong all along about how we are managing our used vehicle investments? Have we been chasing the wrong rabbit, choosing to manage cars over cash?

In some ways, we haven't been entirely wrong. Despite the collective lack of used vehicle investment management acumen among dealers and managers, dealers have done pretty well in their used vehicle departments over the years. Take the $1,800 gross example noted previously. Even though it represents the least return on investment (ROI) among the three examples, the $1,800 represents a 73 percent annualized return.

By almost anyone's estimation, that's a pretty good ROI. But it's not the most optimal or profitable ROI the $20,000 investment could achieve. In addition, as I outline in subsequent chapters, I don't think making a mere $1,800 front-end gross profit will be sustainable for two reasons: First, the cost of used vehicles will continue to go up. Second, the retail and wholesale markets will continue to become more efficient. When these forces converge, the average gross profits dealers achieve will shrink and ROI will fall over time. Even if dealers manage to maintain an $1,800 front-end gross in future years, it will require investing even more money to achieve it, which translates to less ROI.

The good news, however, is that we now understand how dealers and their managers can become better managers of their used vehicle investments. My intent in writing this book is to help dealers understand why it's imperative to adopt an investment- or ROI-minded approach to used vehicle inventory management right now and detail the right way to do it.

The book reflects my best understanding of how dealers can build this investment management competency for themselves and their used vehicle teams. It showcases how investment management technology has evolved to give dealers and managers the tools they need to apply prudent investment management principles to their everyday used vehicle decisions.

This book likely won't be an easy read for some. In fact, it may scare some readers. Why? Because the only way dealers and managers can achieve, or even aspire, to become better ROI-focused managers of their used vehicle investments goes directly to rethinking their identity and purpose within the walls of the used vehicle department and dealership. Simply put, you'll need to find a way to trust the data and insights that are now available to help you make financially prudent decisions in ways you haven't needed to in the past. You'll have to let go of some of the long-held beliefs about what you currently regard as "best practices" for used vehicle inventory management. You'll have to operate outside your current comfort zone. You'll need to remember that your primary purpose isn't just to sell cars, it's to generate a net profit or ROI on every vehicle you manage.

My sincere hope is that this book helps ease your transition by giving you a clear understanding of why ROI-based used vehicle investment management represents a better way forward for the future and showcasing how to get there and stay there.

Thank you for your interest in what I have to say. Enjoy the read.

PART I

SEARCHING FOR A SOLUTION

CHAPTER 1

A TURNING POINT FOR USED VEHICLE PROFITABILITY

Few would argue that dealers enjoyed the best of all worlds in used vehicles in 2021 and 2022.

Yes, it was sometimes difficult to acquire inventory. But when you had the cars, you didn't face much risk. Retail demand was surprisingly strong and used vehicle supplies were limited. This combination caused vehicle values to appreciate week-over-week for extended periods of time.

As a result, the net profit outcomes in used vehicles climbed to unprecedented levels. Dealers could put almost any retail price on any used vehicle and it would sell. Customers, to almost everyone's surprise, would often pay more for a used vehicle than a comparable new one because new vehicles were also in short supply.

Used vehicle gross profits during this go-go era effectively went off the charts. If you look at the average front-end grosses the public dealer groups achieved in 2021 and 2022, you'd see a significant upward spike. In the years prior to the pandemic, the collective average for the public dealer groups hovered around $1,500/car. In 2021 and 2022, the front-end gross average ran close to $2,500/car, with some making even more.

Private dealers enjoyed a similar boon. I had countless conversations with dealers who readily shared stories of consistent $3,000, $4,000, and $5,000 gross profit deals. Add in all the F&I (financing and insurance) money that dealers made during this time, and you've got the makings of a net profit boom in used vehicles that fed an unprecedented rise in overall net profitability for the dealership. It wasn't uncommon for dealers who had consistently achieved a 2 percent to 3 percent overall net profit, or return on sales, for their dealerships prior to the pandemic to book two to three times those amounts. Not surprisingly, this spate of higher-than-ever ROI for dealerships subsequently fed a historic rise in the number of buy/sell deals for our industry. If you were a dealer who had been waiting for the right moment for your exit, you had it. If you were a dealer wanting to grow your business even more, you had the cash to make it happen.

But while the resiliency of the car business had proven itself once again, a darker undercurrent gained momentum in 2023 and 2024 and continues to grow. This undercurrent represents a significant, even unprecedented, ROI risk for dealers in their used vehicle departments. In fact, as I explain in a moment, this undercurrent has morphed into what appears to be a permanent, foundational change in the used vehicle ROI equation. Most disturbing, however, is the fact that many dealers, while they may sense the growing pressure on used vehicle profitability and ROI, are completely unaware of the change. Even worse, they are woefully unprepared to meet this challenge to at least preserve and protect the used vehicle ROI potential that is still at hand.

To understand how the ROI imperative has changed in used vehicles, let's examine the chart that compiles figures from Cox Automotive, public dealer group financials, and related ROI calculations (Table 1.1). The ROI tallies assume the average used vehicle retailed in 45 days.

When I look at the chart, the first thing I see likely jives with the first takeaway for every reader—the average front-end gross. While the averages on the chart may not match the gross profits individual dealers achieved over the last decade, they are directionally accurate.

The upshot: By the end of 2023, even after gross profits had

Table 1.1. Cox Automotive ROI calculations

Year	Average wholesale price*	Average front-end gross	ROI
2014	$11,448	$1,720	124.3%
2019	$12,848	$1,432	90.3%
2023	$21,072	$1,911	73.6%
2025	$23,000	$1,800	63.0%

Source: Cox Automotive data and public dealer group SEC filings
*Average wholesale price reflects annualized average purchase prices at Manheim auctions; the figures do not reflect dealers' true investments costs, which typically include auction fees, reconditioning, and other expenses dealers often allocate to each vehicle.

diminished from their historic highs between 2021 and 2022, dealers were booking more gross profit per vehicle than they achieved in 2014 and 2019. That's good news. It's exactly what you'd expect to see in any profit-positive business. In fact, some dealers likely take great comfort in the fact that as they've been retailing vehicles over the years, their gross profits look better over time.

As I'm writing in 2024, I suspect the average $1,911 gross profit the public groups achieved in 2023 is buoyed, at least in part, by post-pandemic after-effects of limited used vehicle supplies and resilient retail demand. I would add that if your current front-end gross profit average meets or exceeds this amount, you should consider yourself fortunate. The figure is higher than the current front-end averages I've been hearing from dealers in my conversations.

But here's where I believe the dark undercurrent, and its impact on used vehicle ROI, really begins to manifest. Take a look at the average wholesale cost of vehicles between 2014 and 2023 on the chart.

In 2014, the average wholesale cost of vehicles—a figure that reflects average wholesale purchase prices at Manheim and not the full investment cost, including reconditioning, that dealers put on their books—was $11,448. By 2019, the wholesale price average had climbed to $12,848, a fairly normal rate of increase over a five-year period.

But look what happened between 2019 and 2023: The average wholesale price rose 64 percent, to $21,072, the highest in the history of the car business.

Now, let's consider how the rising cost of goods sold in used vehicles has reshaped ROI over the years. In 2014, dealers achieved an ROI of 124.3 percent, selling vehicles with an average cost of $11,448 and grossing an average of $1,760. By 2023, dealers achieved the highest front-end gross profit average of $1,911 but the ROI had declined to 73.6 percent.

Now, let's look forward to what we may face in 2025. It's fair to assume, I think, that the average gross profit dealers can achieve will be less than 2023, given the evidence of gross profit declines I hear from dealers. It's also fair to assume that the average wholesale cost for used vehicles will be higher in 2025, given the ever-higher costs of new vehicles sold in recent years.

So, if we presume that the average cost of vehicles will be $23,000 in 2025, and that these investments will generate an average front-end gross of $1,800, the ROI these vehicles produce will be 63 percent—even less than dealers achieved in 2023.

Do you see what's happening here? It's a portrait of used vehicle ROI in decline. It's an illustration of how the ROI imperative for dealers has changed. We now have ever-higher costs of used vehicles generating ever-smaller front-end grosses, a dynamic that inevitably causes ROI to diminish.

If we think of the cost of goods sold in used vehicles as the floor for ROI, and the retail market as the ceiling, dealers are effectively caught in a big ROI squeeze. They must invest ever-larger sums of money in each used vehicle, while the rising efficiency and transparency of both the retail and wholesale markets makes it ever more difficult to generate the gross profits they once enjoyed.

Through this lens, it seems apparent to me that the pandemic, and the high-flying years it spawned in used vehicles, amounted to a reprieve from the advance of used vehicle margin pressures that had taken hold in earnest in the years leading up to 2020. I also believe, given the way used vehicle ROI is now under pressure from both the wholesale and retail sides of the market, the grosses dealers achieved in the pre-pandemic years of 2018 and 2019 may well be the true mark of where future gross profits will go.

How could that be, you might ask? Well, this dynamic of margin compression is exactly what happens in any business when the market becomes more efficient and transparent. It's the nature of our world where new technologies and tools bring ever-greater efficiency and transparency to the way we live and do business.

I realize this outlook might strike normally optimistic dealers as dark and glum. But I would ask: What evidence suggests the outcome will be any different? After all, margin compression always follows market efficiency and transparency.

Given the circumstances, the big question for dealers seems obvious: How can we best manage our used vehicle departments given these less favorable and uncertain market conditions? The answer, I believe, rests with doing the very thing we haven't done as dealers since the day the first used vehicle retailed—operating our used vehicle departments with an eye on the ROI for every investment.

That's why I believe our industry is at a turning point. The time has arrived for dealers to become more astute financial managers of their used vehicle investments if they hope to chart a path to sustained, profitable success in their used vehicle departments.

This belief isn't borne out of thin air. Rather, it comes from a data-science-based exploration of why, in the years prior to the pandemic, dealers were retailing ever-larger numbers of used vehicles and losing money. This exploration has led me to the understanding that, while dealers never really needed to worry about used vehicle ROI in years past, now they do.

Let's have a look at how I, and a team of data scientists at Cox Automotive, arrived at this critically important understanding.

CHAPTER 2

A LOW MOMENT AND RENEWED PURPOSE

I still remember the buzz-kill that happened right around Christmas in 2017.

The holidays are my favorite time of year. I'm a near-Christmas baby, which means my birthday typically marks the start of our annual family gathering and, in recent years, trips to places that give us a chance to recharge and spend as much time together with each other as we can stand.

But the spirit of the holiday season in 2017 crashed when I got a phone call from a dealer who, at that time, owned a very large dealer group in the Northeast. He'd just wrapped up the group's year-end financial review with his leadership team, and they were puzzled, particularly with the results the financials showed for used vehicles.

Like many of his dealer peers, the dealer's financial review revealed two outstanding numbers. The first covered their average front-end gross profit. The group's average ran about $1,300/vehicle, about $100 less than the average for 2017, but totally in line with the broader industry and 20 Group comparisons. Meanwhile, the group's overall sales volume set a new in-house record—up 1 percent to 3 percent, depending on the rooftop. This achievement also fell into line with the broader industry, which saw a 0.5 percent increase in used vehicle sales volume that year, according to the National Automobile Dealers Association (NADA).

The number that surprised the dealer, and his leadership team, arrived when they examined the net profit the used vehicle department generated for the year. Across a couple dozen stores, they'd lost a nearly seven-figure sum. Their finding didn't make sense. It prompted the dealer's call.

"I don't understand this, Dale. We sold a record volume of vehicles and we lost money. This doesn't add up."

I understood the gravity of the situation. The dealer wouldn't have called me during the holidays unless it was something important. The dealer also had an excellent point. His results did not reflect the industry's experience and history selling used vehicles. Generally speaking, if you sold more cars, you'd make more money.

The call was unsettling. I didn't have a good answer for the dealer, and my promise to follow up after the holidays did nothing to ease the dealer's own disappointment and dismay. I also felt like I needed to know more. Was the dealer's experience an anomaly or a canary in the coal mine?

I carried this question with me through the holidays, which made them less fulfilling and satisfying than usual.

When I returned to work in early 2018, the answer came fast.

In call after call with dealers, in the first full week of January, I heard the same or similar story: "WTF? We had a record year in used vehicles and we lost money?"

At the time, margin compression was a big topic of discussion. It was the go-to explanation for the continued decline in average front-end gross profit that dealers experienced in the years following the Great Recession of 2008. Today, we know the decline was a result of broader market forces: The rise of the internet and new technologies brought greater efficiency and transparency to the used vehicle market. Customers were smarter. The vast majority of dealers were using technology and tools to price their used vehicles, enabling everyone to understand how everyone else priced their used vehicles. Competition was fierce. Big grosses still happened, of course, but not in the numbers or scale dealers enjoyed a few years earlier.

But margin compression didn't fully explain why, as NADA later reported in its annual profile of dealership financials, that dealers sold more vehicles in 2017 and achieved a –$2 in average net profit per used vehicle retailed. By the time the report came out, I was extremely troubled by the frequency of dealers sharing their concerns that, while they were doing everything they could to turn vehicles as quickly as possible to mitigate the effects of margin compression, they ended up losing money. It was as if all the hard work and successes they thought they'd achieved suddenly evaporated.

All this led me to the lowest point of my professional career. Every one of the dealers who shared their money-losing stories used the inventory management solution, vAuto, that I brought to the market a decade earlier. Many dealers regarded themselves as

"Velocity" dealers. That is, they subscribed to the Velocity Method of Management philosophy I introduced with vAuto: To get the most out of your used vehicle department, you need to turn every vehicle as quickly as possible to maximize the total gross profit you could make in used vehicles, service, and F&I—and make deals in your new vehicle department.

The dealers' loyalty to vAuto and Velocity principles owed to the success it helped them achieve in the years leading up to 2017. For some, vAuto and Velocity turned the used vehicle department into a lifeline for the dealership. At the time, new vehicles were a loss leader, and factories were pumping more new vehicles into the market. If the dealers had not adopted the philosophy and software I'd introduced, which ignited their used vehicle performance, they might have gone out of business.

Some blamed this turn-and-earn approach, as well as vAuto and me, for creating a "race to the bottom" in used vehicles. While I understood that neither I nor vAuto created the race to the bottom, which is ultimately a byproduct of an ever more efficient and transparent market, I also knew that we likely helped accelerate the pace of market efficiency and transparency, and the resulting used vehicle margin pressures.

For a time, I entered what I now call my "dark period." I gave serious thought to hanging up my professional hat. I thought it might be best to let someone else solve the net profit problem that had taken over the industry. Meanwhile, I would ride off into the sunset with my professional relationships and reputation intact. If people blamed me for the problem after I'd retired, that'd be okay.

But I don't walk away from a problem; when I encounter a

problem, particularly one I may have had a hand in creating, I walk to it.

I also understood that any success I'd achieved in the car business, which has provided my family and me with more blessings than we can count, was owed to dealers, like the one who called me during the holidays in 2017 and those who came to me for explanations and ways to address the decreasing net profitability they were achieving in used vehicles.

In the end, I felt a deep sense of obligation and responsibility to see if (a) I could understand the root causes of the net profit deficiencies that had become the norm for dealers and (b) if the vAuto team and I might be able to offer a better solution.

This sense of personal accountability and responsibility led me to make two phone calls in the spring of 2018. The first went to the head of Cox Automotive at the time, Sandy Schwartz. He knew I was contemplating retirement. I laid out my plan to get to the bottom of the net profit problem. I was brutally honest. I told him I didn't know if we'd find a solution, and if we did, it might be very disruptive for our business. He understood the implications and, more importantly, shared my belief that we owed it to our dealer-clients to do the investigative work and find a better way, if one even existed.

My second call would eventually go to Chris Stutsman, a brilliant developer with a deep understanding of data science. Chris was an architect behind vAuto at its inception. He's the guy who helped develop the models and methods that enabled us to render market data to help dealers manage their used vehicle inventories more effectively.

I planned to ask for Chris's help to test a hunch that, despite all the external factors driving market efficiency and transparency, something wasn't right in the way dealers managed their used vehicle inventories. My hunch followed an examination of the traditional used vehicle playbook that dealers and our industry had used for decades. My examination revealed a curious finding. The next chapter spells it out.

CHAPTER 3

A HUNCH: SOMETHING'S MISSING IN THE USED VEHICLE PLAYBOOK

During my dark period, I turned the traditional used vehicle playbook inside and out. I was desperate to find something—anything—that might offer a clue as to how and why dealers were selling more used vehicles and losing money.

I also studied the businesses of retailers who were super-keen on inventory management and who weren't immune from the rising tide of technology-driven efficiencies and resulting pressure on profit margins that dealers faced in the prior decade. Somewhere along the way (and I can't recall any specific inspiration), I realized that other retailers focused a great deal of management time and attention on their return on investment (ROI).

In their financials and earnings calls, company executives would highlight how they worked to maximize ROI on their inventory assets. They cared about an inventory unit's cost, and how long it sat in their inventory or on a shelf, before they sold it and realized a return. I then reflected on how rarely, if ever, ROI came up in my conversations with dealers about their used vehicle businesses.

We might examine a vehicle that hadn't sold in 45 or 60 days. We'd look at the reasons the vehicle's cost might be too high, and how a manager handled the vehicle's pricing over the past 30 days. We'd zero in on process problems—like a vehicle's high cost owing to an appraisal bump, or an unexpectedly high cost for reconditioning. We'd look at the way a manager initially priced a vehicle and how much they paid attention to the vehicle's retail pricing while they owned it. We'd talk about how the dealer would need to discount the price if they truly wanted to sell the car.

All of these conversations fell squarely into the principles of Velocity management. They were aimed at helping dealers understand the need to turn vehicles more quickly, and to be extremely careful and realistic about vehicles that suffered from someone overpaying for a unit and someone else trying to pass the problem along to a buyer.

But nowhere in the conversations that I recalled did we ever talk about ROI. Looking back, I started to realize that the absence of ROI in these discussions might reflect the fact that ROI wasn't a part of the used vehicle playbook. It wasn't a top-of-mind operational principle for me, or the dealers and their used vehicle managers.

This realization turned into a hunch that perhaps the used vehicle playbook was missing a critical element that, had it been present, might have meant less pressure on used vehicle margins and profitability, even with the rise of new technologies and ever-greater levels of market efficiency and transparency. I then tested my hunch with colleagues and dealer friends. I'd ask, "Why is it that every other industry, especially retail businesses, make ROI a fundamental part of their operational priorities? Why don't we do this in used vehicles, despite dealers investing millions, even tens of millions, of dollars in their inventories?"

Whenever I raised the question, I'd get a similar answer: "Dale, we do care about ROI. That's how we determine if we make money when we move a car."

I'd push back. "Okay," I'd say. "If that's the case, let me ask a couple questions. First, if you made a $2,500 gross on the retail sale of a used vehicle, you'd think it was a pretty good outcome, right?" Almost every dealer with whom I posed the question would agree.

Next, I'd ask. "Okay, what if you made the $2,500 on a $50,000 vehicle that took 60 days to sell, and you made $2,500 on a $15,000 vehicle that took 20 days to sell. Would the $2,500 for each deal represent the same ROI?"

Dealers would acknowledge that of course not. The $2,500 profit on a $15,000 vehicle that took 20 days to sell would represent a far better return on investment.

Then, I'd come in for the close: "If you looked at your sales log tomorrow and saw two $2,500 deals, would you then ask, 'How much did we invest in the vehicle?' and 'How long did it take us to sell it?'"

Dealers would admit, often reluctantly, that they didn't ask those questions. These ROI-minded queries—how much did you invest in a vehicle, how long did it take to sell, and how much money did you make when it sold?—were never part of the sales log analysis. They were also never part of the weekly used vehicle sales meetings.

Such conversations led to my call with vAuto's Chris Stutsman. He and his team proved to be the first of two advantages I enjoyed at the time. Chris was part of a growing group of data scientists that Cox Automotive and vAuto employed to gather, analyze, and refine the market and dealership performance data that powers our solutions.

My second advantage came as a benefit of working with vAuto and Cox Automotive. Thanks to a decade of helping dealers manage their used vehicle inventories, we had access to several million historical used vehicle transactions. We knew how much dealers paid for their vehicles, how long it took to sell them, and how much money they made when the vehicles sold. In other words, we had the foundational elements we needed to assess whether the absence of ROI in the dealers' playbook could be part of the profitability problem that had come to define the used vehicle business.

When I got Chris on the phone, he agreed that my hunch was worth the data science exploration. As a first step, though, Chris and his team recommended that we first determine the characteristics and factors of specific vehicles that drive ROI, an exercise that proved to be challenging. The next chapter tells the story.

PART II

THE PATH OF SCIENCE-DRIVEN DISCOVERY

CHAPTER 4

AN EFFORT TO UNDERSTAND WHAT DRIVES USED VEHICLE ROI

When Chris and I set out to understand the elements that drive used vehicle ROI, I had no idea how much the effort would turn into an education about the basics of the used car business and hardcore data science.

Going into the ROI exploration, we knew a couple of things.

First, we knew we'd need to establish how we'd define the ROI for a used vehicle. For this exercise, we applied the fundamental elements that determine a used vehicle's ROI. We agreed that there are three—the investment amount of the vehicle, the retail gross profit generated at the time of the vehicle's sale, and the length of time it took to sell the vehicle and realize the vehicle's gross profit return.

Chris and his team applied the math to the millions of historic used vehicle transactions in the vAuto database. They ended up grouping vehicles into three categories—those with high ROI, medium ROI, and low ROI.

I found it interesting, and somewhat promising, that our ROI analyses ended up looking a lot like dealer inventories I'd seen over the years. The individual ROI buckets the team produced weren't equal in share or size. It wasn't like dealers were sitting on piles of high-ROI vehicles. Rather, the groupings reflected the variability of the used vehicle business itself, and the distinct ways dealers manage their used vehicles differently. In the end, high-ROI vehicles accounted for roughly 20 percent of the overall total of historic vehicle transactions. Medium-ROI vehicles accounted for about 35 percent, while low-ROI vehicles accounted for roughly 45 percent of the total.

But while I found this finding interesting, it only moved us a small step closer toward our goal of determining the characteristics that drive a used vehicle's ROI performance. Chris and his data science team built a set of several hundred distinct characteristics that they believed would have at least some influence on a used vehicle's ROI outcome.

The characteristics covered all the things you'd expect—color, condition, equipment, mileage, and so on. Chris and his team also accounted for the fact that the same or similar vehicle, owned and then retailed by two separate dealers, could have significantly different ROI outcomes. The data science work at this stage of our research effort included identifying, tracking, and assessing how much influence a distinct, individual factor about a vehicle might have on its ROI outcome.

I won't bore you with all the details. Suffice it to say this data science work took several months with Chris and his team constantly testing and retesting their assumptions and findings against our database of historic transactions. The end goal was to determine, in a scientific and statistically meaningful way, the factors that had the greatest impact or influence on a vehicle's ROI outcome.

During this period, I had to dig deep and find the patience to let Chris and his team do their work. I was hungry for answers. More than once, I had to be reminded that, like fine wine, statistically solid data science takes time—and perhaps I should just have a glass.

After what seemed like an eternity, Chris called me one day to share the news. He and his data science team had done all the hardcore number-crunching and analysis to determine the three factors that, across the millions of historic used vehicle transactions in our database, had the highest statistical correlation to producing ROI outcomes.

I wasn't surprised at all when Chris shared the three factors, and I suspect no one reading this book will be surprised either. The factors the data science produced were intuitively obvious—so much so that we wondered why we hadn't figured it out earlier. But we all knew another truth: Without the team of data scientists, and the technologies that enabled us to wrangle science-backed insights from a mountain of data, we'd have only been guessing.

The following are the factors that have the highest statistical correlation to a used vehicle's ROI.

Cost to Market: As it turns out, the first characteristic of a vehicle that has a high statistical correlation to its ROI outcome is its Cost to Market. That makes intuitive sense to everyone in the used car business. The more right you own a car, the more likely you are to make a larger gross profit. And gross profit is one of the three elements, along with how much money invested in a vehicle and how long you had to hold the investment, that make up a vehicle's ROI.

Market Days Supply: The second of the many characteristics that had a statistically high correlation to ROI is Market Days Supply. This finding also makes sense. When you have a vehicle with high demand and low supply, you often don't have to discount the vehicle or discount it as much to sell it. Such conditions frequently lead to a higher gross profit, which is one of the three elements that determines ROI.

Retail volume: The third characteristic that Chris and his team found to have a high statistical correlation to determine ROI is the popularity of the vehicle in a market as measured by its retail volume. That's intuitive, too. Generally speaking, popular vehicles are likely to move faster than less-popular vehicles—a factor that can contribute positively to a vehicle's speed of turn, one of the three ROI elements.

Once the data science team determined that these three characteristics were the most statistically significant in shaping the ROI outcome for every used vehicle, Chris and his team invented a scoring system that would reflect the varying levels of ROI that tend to occur across all used vehicles. I share more about the scoring system, and the insights its application yielded, in the next chapter.

At this point, I was excited to finally know that our data science work had produced a tangible result. I was also curious. I asked Chris and his team to apply their ROI algorithm and scoring system to vAuto's live database. I wanted to test the validity of the three ROI factors against vehicles currently in the market. I wanted to watch and see how their ultimate ROI outcomes compared to our predictions.

Here, we hit a significant bump. Looking back, I guess you could say we were being naïve. We thought that applying Cost to Market, Market Days Supply, and retail volume in equal measure to every car would be sufficient to determine a specific vehicle's ROI potential.

Boy, we were so wrong. It didn't take long for us to figure out that the three ROI factors *do not* apply in equal weight or measure to every vehicle. In fact, each factor varies, in measure and weight, from car to car.

We figured out pretty quickly that we had a whole lot more data science ahead of us. In fact, it took us the better part of a year to determine exactly how much weight should be given to each ROI factor for each individual vehicle, at any particular moment in time.

During these months, I thought of the prophet Job and tried to summon his patience. I certainly hoped Chris and his team could figure out the complex problem we'd set out to solve. But I wasn't really sure.

Finally, in the fall of 2018, I got word. The ROI algorithm that Chris and his team produced was, in fact, capable of accurately predicting and scoring the ROI outcome of any vehicle approximately 90 percent of the time. Our findings were irrefutable, thanks to the data science team's testing and retesting of results, and continual adjustments to the algorithm and investment scoring system, against vehicles in vAuto's live database.

This work led me to ask Chris and his team to apply the algorithm and investment scoring system in a different way. We'd been evaluating the accuracy and efficacy of the algorithm and scoring system on a car-by-car basis. We had been applying the investment scoring system to individual vehicles and watching to see if our score proved to be an accurate and reliable predictor of a vehicle's ROI outcome when it sold.

Now, I was curious to see what we'd find if we rolled up all the vehicles in vAuto's live database as if they represented a single dealer's inventory. Several million vehicles, one big inventory. My goal was to prove or disprove my hunch that dealers did not, in fact, make pricing decisions based on a vehicle's ROI potential. This exercise proved to be affirming and deeply disturbing.

But before we go there, it's important to understand the nature of our new used vehicle investment scoring system and what its application across individual vehicles revealed about the absence of ROI-minded management in the traditional used vehicle playbook.

CHAPTER 5

GOING FULL CIRCLE TO SCORE USED VEHICLES

Not many people remember how vAuto got started. The truth is, it came out of a business idea that, I thought, had a lot of merit for the industry—scoring individual used vehicles on a scale of 1–100 so dealers would have a way to know if someone paid too much for a vehicle and they might now have a problem car in their inventory.

This original scoring system was a central feature of mPower Auto, the company that launched in 2003 and, over time, became vAuto. Here's how mPower worked: Using a mobile phone, mPower users could appraise a vehicle, entering a vehicle identification number (VIN) number that prompted our system to look up the dealer's valuation guide of choice (i.e., Black Book, Galves, Kelley Blue Book, etc.). The system would score a vehicle based on how well their appraisal or purchase amount aligned to a book value.

Some dealers loved mPower. I distinctly recall former Polar Chevrolet dealer Bill Krouse, who was one of the industry's first one-price dealers, saying he appreciated mPower's ability to help him buy vehicles more consistently on the money. This ability was critical—at a one-price store where your prices often lead the market, your retail pricing strategy suffers if you don't buy the cars right.

Then there were dealers like Ed Napleton in Chicago. I remember the flurry of calls I received from Ed during a son's birthday party on a Saturday afternoon. He absolutely loved the fact that mPower would send him a text to tell him when an appraiser had put too much money into a vehicle.

But the primary idea behind mPower's scoring system was to give dealers, at the moment of decisioning, a view of how "right" they were acquiring cars. The system worked well enough, but the rise of the internet eventually led to vAuto—a solution that mined the *retail* market for data to guide appraising and pricing decisions. With vAuto, we were still providing guidance to help dealers make better decisions, but we got out of the business of scoring vehicles, in part because wholesale valuations were less relevant. We also knew that our ability to render retail market data, as the internet was ushering in a higher level of two-way pricing transparency, proved to be a significant value-add for dealers who used it.

Fast-forward 15 years. I realized that when Chris and his team had invented a scoring system to capture a used vehicle's ROI potential, it had brought me full circle. Here we were, long after mPower had pivoted to become vAuto, scoring vehicles again.

The new scoring system provides a clear, understandable breakdown of the wide range of potential ROI that exists across a dealer's inventory—a vehicle-specific view of ROI potential within the three inventory-level buckets of low, medium, and high ROI that Chris and his team created. They understood, for example, that the retail gross profit dealers achieved on high-ROI vehicles could differ by several thousand dollars even within the same high-ROI bucket.

Therefore, the team devised a 1–12 scoring system, wherein vehicles with the highest ROI potential scored at the top of the 12-point scale, and vehicles with the least ROI potential ranked at the bottom. The 12-point scale also prompted us to create a way of classifying the scores that conveyed the gradient range of ROI outcomes. After some discussion, we agreed that using precious metals made good sense. Dealers would intuitively understand that Bronze, Silver, Gold, and Platinum designations represented progressively better ROI outcomes.

Here's a quick rundown of the scoring system: The Platinum vehicles, the ones that score between 10 and 12, are the ones for which we can predict with almost absolute certainty that when they retail, they will achieve among the highest returns on investment. These are vehicles that are characterized by low Cost to Market, the fact that the dealer owns the car really right, low Market Days Supply, and high retail volume.

On the opposite end of the spectrum, the Bronze vehicles are the ones for which we can predict with almost absolute certainty that when they retail, they will achieve little if any return on investment and, sometimes, a negative return on investment. Bronze vehicles are the ones that have a high Cost to Market. The dealer owns them for a lot of money—maybe too much. They have a high Market Days Supply and low retail volume.

It should be noted that within these precious metal buckets the return on investment for a specific vehicle depends on its score. With Platinum vehicles, a unit that scores a 12 will have a better ROI than a vehicle that scores a 10. In the Bronze category, a vehicle that scores a 3 will have a better ROI than a vehicle that scores a 1.

I have to admit: The scoring system Chris and his team created outshines anything we did with mPower. Back then, we scored a dealer's appraisal/purchase price against a book value. That's easy compared to doing all the data science to determine the precise elements that drive a used vehicle's ROI potential and then producing a reliably predictive score on its eventual retail outcome.

In many ways, the new ROI-predictive scoring system for used vehicles we developed would not have been possible in the mPower days. The machine-learning-oriented technology and tools that power today's data science didn't exist.

But that was then, and this is now. When Chris and his team showed me what they'd created, I knew we were onto something. I also knew we had one more significant thing to prove—that, despite what they believed or claimed to believe, dealers were not managing their used vehicle inventories to maximize the ROI of each vehicle. I needed to know if our investment scoring system would confirm or refute my hunch.

I needed to ask Chris and his team to do one more thing and, when they did, I knew that I wasn't ready to retire. I also knew we had discovered a new, better way to manage used vehicles that I believed, over time, would take hold in every dealership.

CHAPTER 6

THE SHOCKING MOMENT OF DISCOVERY

In late 2018, after Chris and his team had proven our ability to accurately predict a used vehicle's ROI potential and provide an investment score, I asked them to give me a different view of our data.

As I noted earlier, we'd been scoring individual vehicles in vAuto's live database of several million vehicles. This effort was essential to prove our ROI-prediction capability.

But I had something different in mind. I wanted to see what we'd find if we viewed all the vehicles in vAuto's database as if they made up a single large dealership or enterprise. I wanted to further test whether dealers were or weren't, as a whole, applying ROI-minded principles to their used vehicle management decisions.

I've included the composite view of the multimillion-vehicle inventory Chris and his team developed (Table 6.1). The composite hit me like a ton of bricks. I couldn't believe what I was seeing.

Table 6.1. National averages

	Percentage of vehicles	Average Price to Market	Average Cost to Market	Average Market Days Supply	Average age
Platinum	19%	96.4%	81.4%	48	35
Gold	29%	97.4%	88.0%	68	39
Silver	25%	99.0%	93.5%	70	47
Bronze	28%	101.0%	100.4%	74	81

When I share the composite with dealers, there are two things that should absolutely jump off the page and strike anyone who's been in the car business for more than a minute as patently irrational.

The first thing is the Bronze cars, which run from left to right at the bottom of the chart. These are the vehicles dealers own for the most amount of money, maybe too much money, as evidenced by their average Cost to Market percentage of slightly more than 100 percent. They are the vehicles with the highest Market Days Supply (74) and the lowest retail volume. And yet, in spite of these unfortunate characteristics, these are the vehicles dealers have priced the highest, or most proudly. It's as if dealers treat them like fine wine and believe they will get better over time. It's as if dealers believe they are worth keeping around. We all know this isn't true. This just doesn't make any sense.

The second jump-off-the-page takeaway comes with the Platinum vehicles, which sit at the opposite end of the spectrum compared to the Bronze vehicles. The Platinum vehicles are the ones that the dealers own for the least amount of money (a Cost to Market of 81.4 percent), have the lowest Market Days Supply (48), and are the most popular, high-volume sellers in the market. And yet, despite these favorable characteristics, dealers are pricing their Platinum vehicles as if they are distressed and need to be blown out yesterday—something that simply doesn't make any sense.

When I saw the composite, I was blown away. Nobody who's spent more than a minute in the car business can look at the composite, see the way dealers are treating their Platinum and Bronze vehicles, and defend it as a rational, ROI-minded approach to managing used vehicles. Everybody who's got some car business experience knows dealers should be treating these vehicles exactly the opposite. Everybody knows we should be most proud of the Platinum vehicles, pricing them less aggressively to make the gross they deserve, while applying the highest amount of urgency to the Bronze vehicles to move them faster.

But while the composite revealed an alarming lack of ROI sensitivity and understanding across all of the vehicles in vAuto's live database, I understood it didn't fully prove my hunch that, despite what they believe and say, dealers do not account for an individual vehicle's ROI as they manage used vehicles.

That's why I asked Chris and his team to show me how many of the approximately 12,000 dealers we served had a rational pricing profile. In other words, I wanted to know how many were pricing their Platinum vehicles the highest and showing the greatest amount of urgency in pricing their Bronze vehicles to move them quickly. I thought that if we found any dealers with an investment-rational pricing profile, I needed to talk to them and understand how they came to understand that ROI matters in used vehicles.

But when Chris came back with the answer in late 2018, that's the moment I knew two things were true. I wasn't ready to retire and I knew that what we'd discovered would change the way every dealer managed used vehicles. I knew this because the answer, shockingly, was zero. None. Not a single dealer among the approximately 12,000 dealers the composite represented had a rational pricing profile.

Naturally, this discovery and proof point led me to a host of other questions. How can this be? How can it possibly be true that every dealer effectively manages their used vehicle in exactly the same way, especially in a manner that no one could explain or rationalize?

I answer these questions in a bit. First, though, it's important to take a slightly deeper dive into what we've discovered about the nature of time in used vehicles and how bananas reveal where we've all been wrong.

CHAPTER 7

HOW BANANAS PARTLY EXPLAIN OUR IRRATIONAL PRICING PROFILE PROBLEM

Since the dawn of the used vehicle business, dealers have generally understood that time is the enemy of used vehicle profitability. Over time, we all understand that the cost we paid for a used vehicle investment doesn't change, but its market value changes.

In other words, the clock is always ticking on every car. This reality is precisely the reason that dealers often implement inventory age policies that call for moving vehicles out after 45, 60, or even 90 days.

But underneath this understanding that time eventually erodes the profitability of vehicles is the belief in the traditional used vehicle playbook that every vehicle deserves at least some time to make gross. That is, on Day 1, every vehicle possesses its maximum profit potential. Our ROI research, however, indicates this simply isn't true given the way vehicles arrive in dealer inventories today.

A good way to explain this new-found understanding about the nature of time in used vehicles relates to bananas and the way they ripen and grow rotten over time. I've incorporated this analogy into a video I share during my presentations with dealers. The following is a transcript of the video, and Figure 7.1 is the QR code that will give you access to the video to follow along.

> Let's imagine a banana. We can all understand the ripeness of a banana, that it goes through stages over time.
>
> On Day 1, it's a green banana. Full of potential, with lots of time ahead.
>
> A few days pass, and you have a perfectly ripe banana. It's in its prime. But it won't stay like this forever.

Figure 7.1. QR code to "How Bananas Reflect Used Vehicle Investment Value" video

Because a few more days go by, and then you have a bruised banana.

I mean, this is not good. Its time is running out and may have already passed.

If you were selling it, you'd give it a heavy discount or expect to throw it out soon.

Because after a few more days pass, things get ugly. You've got a gooey, rotten banana and you've got to get rid of it because it stinks.

Okay, you see where this is going, right? In some ways, cars are like bananas. Profit potential, like ripeness, will diminish over time.

But unfortunately, cars aren't exactly like bananas.

Unfortunately, our challenge is a bit more complex.

For one thing, while most bananas age pretty consistently, different cars age at very different rates from each other.

So imagine two cars, shown here on Day 1, with their profit potential high, represented as green bananas.

By Day 15 in your inventory, the profit potential of both cars settle in. Let's represent this as both cars being perfectly ripe bananas.

But by Day 30, it's not uncommon for one vehicle to hold its potential longer than the other. Here, the first car is holding strong while the second car has become a bruised banana.

And by Day 45, the factors that make that first car a high potential vehicle still remain high. It's still perfectly ripe. While car two, has dropped off the table. It's a gooey, rotten banana on your lot and it's got to go.

So, what does saying that both these cars, at Day 45, tell you about each one's profit potential?

Nothing. Day 45 tells you nothing.

But hold that thought. There's another way the car challenge is more complex.

With cars, you're not always working with a green banana on Day 1.

Bruised. Perfectly ripe. Green. Vehicles can be at any stage when you take them in.

You might even be taking home a gooey, rotten banana on Day 1.

Maybe by accident. But maybe on purposes.

Maybe you chose to buy a rotten banana to close another deal. And if that's the case, what does saying that this car is on Day 1 tell you about the profit potential of that investment?

The answer is nothing. Saying a car is on Day 1 or Day 45 means nothing. The days on the calendar tells you nothing about the profit potential of any given car.

You see the problem in both of these scenarios, and in many scenarios throughout the industry?

The calendar *is* the problem. The calendar is an

> old, crude form of technology and it tells you nothing, nothing, about the value of these investments.
>
> It's a flawed way of thinking about it, left over from a different time.
>
> We may believe it, without even questioning it, but we've got to realize that calendar time does not equal profit potential.

There it is. Calendar time does not equal profit potential. In the next chapter, I explain the first of two reasons why our industry's belief that calendar time serves as a measurement of a used vehicle's profit potential is highly problematic and contributes to suboptimal and often downright irrational inventory management and pricing decisions.

CHAPTER 8

HOW A FLAWED PREMISE HURTS US IN USED VEHICLES

Our new-found understanding about the nature of time in used vehicles leads to an incredibly important question: How can it be that every dealer is pricing their vehicles irrationally, with little or no recognition of their ROI potential?

I've come to understand that there are two reasons for the absence of ROI recognition in used vehicle management today.

The first reason owes to the fact that we've been pricing used vehicles based on a flawed premise—that the days on the calendar equal profit potential. We currently believe that every vehicle that enters our inventory on Day 1 is fresh and full of gross profit potential. We've followed this premise or principle since the dawn of the used vehicle business. I followed it when I was a dealer and, up until now, believed it to be true.

But here's the thing. In business or life, whenever you make decisions based on a flawed premise, the decisions themselves are flawed and their outcomes won't be optimal.

In some ways, it's almost bizarre that in the age of ever-evolving gains in technology-driven efficiency and insights, our industry follows a playbook principle that essentially says, "The number of times the sun, a star in the sky, rises in the east and sets in the west over our used vehicles, as measured by days on the calendar, is somehow an accurate assessment of the amount of opportunity a vehicle holds."

We can now clearly see the fallacy and flaw in this operational principle. One of the most important discoveries we made in determining how to predict a used vehicle's ROI potential came from watching millions of vehicles come and go across live dealership inventories. We saw a consistent, eye-opening trend: More than 50 percent of the time, vehicles entered dealer inventories as brown and rotten bananas on their first day of life in inventory. Such vehicles fit the Silver or Bronze designations in our new ROI measurement system.

But that's not how the individual pricing the vehicles would think about them. For this person, who's more than likely moored in the belief that a fresh vehicle is full of gross and has the benefit of time, the vehicles represent green bananas. Therefore, we should give them time to go for all the gross.

And yet we now know that this calendar-driven approach to pricing vehicles is wrong more than 50 percent of the time.

Of course, the individual pricing your used vehicles probably wouldn't make this mistake if you were selling bananas instead of used vehicles.

Let's say you're selling bananas, and today, you receive a shipment of fresh bananas. You open the box, and much to your surprise, they're not all green bananas. Instead, some bananas are green, some are yellow, some are brown, and some are rotten.

What would you do if you were a prudent, investment-minded businessperson? We all know the answer. You'd be looking to optimize your investment in this fresh inventory. The first thing you'd do is grab the rotten bananas, price them super low to move and put them on the shelf. Your retailing play here would be to appeal to buyers who want rotten bananas to make banana bread.

Next, you'd put the brown bananas on the shelf, pricing them a bit higher than the rotten ones. Then, you'd put the yellow bananas on the shelf at an even higher price. Finally, you'd put the green bananas on the shelf at the highest price, which would be reflective of their higher ROI potential. This is how any prudent, rational businessperson would optimize their investment in this inventory.

Unfortunately, that's exactly the opposite of what we do in the car business. We tend to apply our calendar-based thinking. We'll likely put the same markup on all vehicles on Day 1, irrespective of what their true ROI potential might be. Even worse, we then wonder why, in the margin-compressed days that led up to the pandemic, we were losing money in our used vehicle departments. Today, the answer stands crystal clear—we are all doing it wrong.

I recognize that some readers, especially those who've been around the used vehicle business for decades like me, might be thinking, "Wait a minute, how is it possible that we've made money all these years if we've been doing it wrong?"

It's a fair and valid question. I believe the answer goes to how the used vehicle market used to operate. Before the internet, and even through its early years, the used vehicle market was less efficient and transparent. You might say it was cloudy, and dealers had the clearest view, especially compared to customers. In this environment, there's generally lots of margin opportunity and you can get away with making decisions on a flawed premise and still make good money.

But as the used vehicle business has become an internet business, and the market has become more efficient and transparent, there's less margin opportunity. In this environment, the cost of making used vehicle pricing decisions based on a flawed premise becomes more obvious and painful. Put another way, we could afford to make less effective decisions when the market was less efficient. Unfortunately, that's not the case today—and that's exactly what happened in the years leading up to the pandemic in 2020.

Now, before anyone gets bent out of shape contemplating how much money they *could* have made if the calendar wasn't the primary means of understanding a used vehicle value, it's important to recognize that our ability to identify the flawed premise of the calendar wasn't available until now. This new understanding would not have occurred but for the advancement of data science and related technologies that enabled our ability to ask what truly drives a used vehicle's ROI potential and how we can predict this potential.

Think about it. In ancient times, mariners crossed vast oceans navigating their ships by the stars. Sometimes they made their destination, sometimes they didn't. Sometimes, when they made land, it wasn't the shore where they initially intended or wanted to arrive. Over time, technology advanced and mariners could use a compass to navigate. Crossing oceans became more precise, predictable and safe. Today, virtually every ocean-going vessel is equipped with a global positioning system (GPS) and a weather tracking system, both of which have made navigating oceans even more precise and safe.

But we in the car business are still navigating by the star in the sky called the sun. Just like early mariners, we're measuring the profit potential of every used vehicle by the passing of days on the calendar.

The good news, however, is that the technology and tools that enable a more sophisticated, ROI-based approach to managing used vehicles in today's margin-compressed environment has arrived. The big question is whether we, as long-time practitioners of calendar-based inventory management, are able and willing to change how we think and behave.

This crossroads provides a fitting segue into the second reason every single dealer in the country has a suboptimal and irrational used vehicle pricing profile. Let's go to the next chapter.

CHAPTER 9

HOW HUMAN NATURE HURTS US IN USED VEHICLES

One of the fairly standard features of almost every used vehicle department is that someone is, or should be, in charge of used vehicle pricing decisions.

Generally speaking, this individual is likely a "car person," someone who has built a career around their knowledge of used vehicles and their ability to put "eyes" on every car. This person is also likely the one who makes deals with customers, approves trade-in offers, and lands on a vehicle purchase price with a customer, along with a host of other responsibilities.

The other common feature of these individuals is that they are all human beings. They bring individualized beliefs, biases and emotions to work every day. They also all rely on their brains to make decisions.

Therein lies the second reason every dealer has an irrational, suboptimal used vehicle pricing profile. In addition to making decisions based on a flawed premise, as we discussed in the last chapter, every used vehicle manager's brain reflects one of the most profound aspects of being human: Our brains are wired to avoid pain and loss.

Take a moment to imagine how miserable our lives would be if it were the opposite. That we woke up every morning wired to find or manufacture situations that bring us pain and loss.

The reality, which any behavioral scientist would affirm, is that we tend to do the opposite. We often go to great lengths to avoid pain and loss. While we all don't necessarily seek out happiness, we most certainly don't welcome pain and loss into our lives every day.

Now, let's think about how the wiring of our brains works when it comes to making pricing decisions on used vehicles. Let's imagine that you had the benefit of knowing that when you see a vehicle on its first day of inventory life and you know it was in distress, it was a rotten banana, or a Bronze vehicle.

You'd understand that the vehicle is in distress because you own it for big money, maybe too much money. The vehicle's got a high Market Days Supply and it's a low volume mover in your market.

I know what you'll do in this situation. We all know what anyone would do. You'll say, "Well, let's give it some time. Let's give it a chance."

In addition to the flawed premise that giving every used vehicle more time to earn its "chance," this decision reflects the way our brains are wired. It's human nature to avoid facing the music on a vehicle that's Bronze or in distress on Day 1. Ultimately, we'll follow this human nature and kick the can down the road. You'll price the vehicle as if it wasn't in distress and had all the gross profit potential in the world. Some dealers and managers do this more than others, of course, but that's largely what we do every day in used vehicle departments across the country.

It should be noted, too, that while decisions can be made to address a problem car at a later date, such decisions also reflect past experience.

In the past, the market rewarded us for kicking the can down the road. In previous times, when the market was less transparent, when used vehicle shoppers didn't have all the information they have available today, someone would come along who didn't know any better. They'd pay us too much money and take the vehicle off our hands.

We saw similar rewards during the immediate post-pandemic years. In fact, with the appreciating market we saw in 2021, in 2022, and for stretches in 2023, we earned even bigger rewards than we did years earlier.

Unfortunately, things are different today. Market conditions have normalized. There are fewer naïve or uneducated customers out there to consider kicking the can down the road as a legitimate strategy for success in used vehicles.

So there you have it. The two big reasons every dealer across the country has a suboptimal used vehicle pricing profile are the flawed premise about the calendar and a perfectly understandable human desire to avoid pain and loss.

When I came to understand these two hurdles, and the strength of the data science's ability to predict a used vehicle's ROI potential, I knew that I wasn't ready to retire. I also knew that it wasn't crazy to believe that eventually every dealer will come to the same understanding. Over time, every dealer will begin to think and operate differently in their used vehicle departments. They will leave the calendar behind as a primary means of determining a used vehicle's ROI potential and begin to focus on truly managing the ROI inherent in every used car.

I'm also fully aware that this industry-wide transition will take time. And, it will take some dealers more time than others. Why? Well, even though market conditions are less favorable for dealers and we're seeing renewed pressure on used vehicle margins and ROI, dealers believe they are, by and large, doing as good as (if not better) than they did prior to the pandemic.

Of course, I have a different view. I would argue that dealers would make more money, and retail more used vehicles, if they changed their strategy from managing the time a vehicle stays in inventory to managing the ROI potential each vehicle holds.

The truth, however, is that used vehicle profitability and sales haven't yet diminished to the point where some dealers believe they need to do something differently. I get it. I'm not here to push anyone into something they don't believe is right for their business.

But we're in a cyclical business, and all signs suggest that we're heading back to where we've been, in terms of used vehicle profitability and sales. We may even go back to the way it was between 2017 and 2019, when many dealers were selling record numbers of used vehicles and not making any money.

Maybe that'll be the time that a critical mass of dealers will say, "I'm ready to do something different. I'm ready to put the old playbook and its reliance on the calendar aside."

As I mentioned before, history will ultimately judge whether my claim or prediction that ROI-focused management will be the cornerstone of every successful used vehicle department. As I write today, however, I believe this is how our industry will operate in the years ahead. I can also say that the transition offers dealers a mix of good news and bad news, should they choose to adopt an ROI-focused approach to managing their used vehicle investments.

Let's start with the bad news.

CHAPTER 10

THE BAD NEWS AHEAD FOR DEALERS

While I'm 100 percent confident that over time, dealers will move away from the calendar as a primary means of assessing a used vehicle's potential in favor of managing each used vehicle based on its investment potential, the transition won't be easy.

I say that having spent countless hours working with dealers to become more prudent managers of their used vehicle investments. I've seen their struggles to get their heads around what it truly means when a vehicle arrives as a distressed investment, or a Silver or Bronze vehicle, on Day 1. I've seen them question or even doubt when the data science tells them to hold out for more gross on a Platinum or Gold vehicle.

Put another way, while our new investment value-based management system goes a long way toward helping you/your team move to managing each used vehicle to its fullest ROI potential, the software alone isn't enough.

Our industry's long-standing reliance on the calendar as a primary means of understanding a used vehicle's potential is a difficult problem to correct. Yes, we now have a software solution that can *help* you correctly move to a more investment-minded strategy. But that doesn't change the fact that the real hurdle rests with the people you put in charge of using it.

That's because the shift to manage used vehicles like a prudent investor would manage a portfolio will require you to behave and think differently. This investment value-focused method will ask you to do things in a way that violates what we all have come to learn and regard as good or sound used vehicle management principles. In effect, you and your team will need to adopt a new playbook for managing used vehicle investments, one that often isn't intuitive or in sync with the methods you've been trained to use.

There are many examples you'll encounter that will test your traditional view of used vehicle management when you move to managing your used vehicles as investments rather than merchandise. Let's examine just a few.

Example 1: Let's imagine you come to work today and you have a vehicle that's on its first day of life in your inventory. The vehicle has arrived as a distressed investment, a unit that falls in the Bronze and Silver categories we outline in Chapter 5. Why is the vehicle distressed? It's because you own it for a lot of money—maybe too much money—it's got a high Market Days Supply, and it's a low-volume mover in your market.

As a prudent investor, the smartest thing you could do, at that moment when you're still sipping your coffee and the vehicle's on its first day in your inventory, is to price the vehicle to sell quickly. The problem is that the price required to move the vehicle quickly could be one that produces zero profit or even a loss.

Now, let's ask ourselves a question: If you put a no-profit or losing price on the vehicle on Day 1, would anyone in the dealership come along today and pat you on the back? Would they say, "Great job!"? We all know the answer is no. Instead, they'd ask what's wrong with you, and they'd point out that the car is only a day old. What's more, if you made this investment-prudent decision repeatedly over time, you might even lose your job.

Example 2: You're working a deal at the desk on a vehicle that happens to be a Platinum car. The reason it ranks as Platinum is because you own it for $2,000 under the money. The customer doesn't have a trade and wants nothing to do with your financing and insurance (F&I) office. Now, here comes the customer's last and final offer: The offer amount would mean you make $1,800 in front-end gross.

I suspect nearly everyone reading this book would take the deal, irrespective of the fact that you own the vehicle for $2,000 under the money. Why would you take it? Because that's what we're trained to do as car people. We don't let any deal walk. If there's daylight, you roll the car.

But that's not what a prudent investor would do. If you were this prudent investment-minded manager, you'd respectfully tell the customer, "Thank you, but no thank you." You'd make this decision and let the customer walk because you'd understand that if you were more patient, you'd make $3,000 to $4,000 on the vehicle.

There are many other points of inherent conflict that arise when you shift from focusing on the calendar to directly managing the investment value of individual used vehicles, like a prudent investor. As we point out in subsequent chapters, such conflicts crop up across vehicle acquisition, appraising and pricing. In each of these mission-critical, ROI-influencing areas, there are deep-rooted and long-standing beliefs about what sound used vehicle management practices should be. Across them, we operate with a collective culture that's skewed to tradition. And, as we all know, you can't and won't change your how-you-think-and-operate culture overnight.

Some readers might even know a dealer who's tried vAuto's investment-based strategy and gave up. They probably told you it just doesn't work.

But I would submit that, in almost every case where a dealer said they would don the hat of a prudent investment manager and have their teams do the same, that hat didn't stay on for very long.

Maybe the hat was the wrong style. Maybe it wasn't the best fit. Maybe no one really wanted to wear the hat in the first place.

Whatever the case, if the dealer's honest with themselves, and you, I suspect their failure story has less to do with the data science and functionality of the system that supports an investment-minded management strategy, and much more to do with their inability to shed the weight of the past and what they believe to be the right way to manage used vehicles.

As any prudent and successful investment manager will tell you, it takes practice, time, and trust to understand how to acquire the right assets in your portfolio, bring them into your portfolio for an acceptable cost of goods sold, and get out or hold each investment until its ROI-appropriate time has come to sell it. Some prudent investors will also tell you it takes courage to trust what the data science tells you, even when your experience or instinct suggests a different course. They'll also share that they've had times when, because of their experience and judgment, they knew the most appropriate and right thing to do with an investment was different than what the data science had been telling them.

Such is the nature of the art and science of managing investments, and the art and science of managing *used vehicle investments*, in today's more data-, technology-, and volatility-driven world.

But I can also say that when dealers and managers make this evolutionary shift in thinking and adopt investment-minded best practices as they manage used vehicles, really good things start to happen.

Let's have a look.

CHAPTER 11

THE GOOD NEWS AHEAD FOR DEALERS

To understand the good news that flows to dealers who shift to behaving and thinking like prudent investment managers, let's go back to the composite I share in Chapter 6 (Table 6.1).

When I first showed the composite, we discussed the inverted, irrational pricing profile that's universal for dealers' used vehicle inventories across the country. The composite also revealed another sometimes sobering reality: Dealers typically have a high percentage, often 50–60 percent, or even more, of investment distressed Silver and Bronze vehicle investments in their inventories.

I call this a sobering reality because some dealers think the share of Silver and Bronze vehicle investments is a bad thing. To them, it signals that they effectively have bad vehicles, or bad investments, in their inventory portfolio.

But nothing could be further from the truth. The truth is that the share of Silver and Bronze vehicles in your inventory, no matter the size, is not a sign of bad acquisitions or investments. To be sure, there probably are some bad acquisitions or investments in the bunch. No one's perfect when it comes to acquiring cars.

Instead, it's important for everyone to understand that the preponderance of Silver and Bronze vehicle investments only reflects a simple fact—you happen to have a lot of these vehicles in your portfolio. And guess what? If you look at the composite in Table 6.1, it's plain to see the same is true for everyone else. The average share of Silver and Bronze vehicles typically runs north of 50 percent of a dealer's inventory.

The key takeaway here is that the share of Silver and Bronze vehicle investments in your inventory portfolio, which represent your assets with the least ROI potential, merely reflects the nature of today's more efficient and transparent used vehicle investment market. While it's possible for you to engineer an inventory portfolio that only possesses better-grade, Platinum and Gold vehicle investments, that's not effectively possible or realistic for dealers who rely on certain levels of sales volume and gross to meet their used vehicle department investment objectives. In other words, the Bronze and Silver vehicle investments are just a common characteristic of today's used vehicle market and the investment portfolios dealers hold to play in the market.

Think about it. Is there any auction where you can find a low Market Days Supply vehicle, that has a high sales volume, and get it cheap? We all know the answer. You aren't likely to ever purchase such vehicles from an auction and, if you do, it probably won't happen again any time soon.

The reality though, is that dealers sometimes need to go to

auctions and acquire vehicles to fill holes in their inventories. Almost by definition, when you factor in buy fees, transportation and the informed, competing interests of other bidders, auction vehicles will arrive in your inventory portfolio with less ROI potential than vehicles acquired in other channels.

These days, even trade-in vehicles are sometimes difficult to acquire on the cheap, or as cheaply as dealers used to acquire them with regularity. Today's consumers know what their vehicles are worth. It's not likely that you can get a vehicle with low Market Days Supply and high sales volume and steal it.

The most important point to know about Bronze and Silver vehicles is that there is absolutely no shame whatsoever in having a high percentage of them. The fact is, you can't avoid them.

But it's also important, from the perspective of prudent investment management, that there *is* shame in not recognizing these vehicles for the risk they represent—and treating them the same way any prudent investor would. That is, you get your money out of them as quickly as possible. If you're not doing that, and you're not doing it day in and day out, that's where there should be shame. That's where you're failing to heed the principles of prudent investment management. You can't avoid having Bronze and Silver vehicles, but you can avoid what the calendar suggests you should do with them when they arrive in your inventory.

The proper treatment of your Silver and Bronze vehicles ushers in the first part of the good news that follows when dealers adopt an investment value-based strategy for managing their used vehicle inventories. When you price your Silver and Bronze vehicle investments to move quickly, as prudent investors would, your sales volume will grow. That's because these vehicles, higher risk though they are, represent your volume vehicles, or your "turners."

How and why will this happen? The gains will come from taking the 50-plus percent of your inventory that are Bronze and Silver investments and pricing them as prudent investment managers—to move as quickly as possible.

Now, you might say, "Okay, Dale, if I do that, and price these vehicles to sell, it's going to be painful. I'm going to have a ton of low grosses and more losses than I'd care to see."

My response is that you may be right. But the reality is that you're going to have to face the less-than-optimal results at some point. These vehicles won't go away by themselves. You're eventually going to suffer. The only question you have to answer is, will it hurt you more to do it today or later? Of course, we all know the answer. It will unquestionably hurt more later.

At the same time, the increase in volume won't be all bad. You'll be putting more people through the F&I office. In addition, you're going to replace these vehicles, capture some internal reconditioning gross, and make some of it back.

The second piece of good news is that as your sales volume increases as you move your Silver and Bronze vehicle investments faster, your overall gross profit average, and return on investment, is going to rise. You might be thinking: How is this possible? Isn't there always a trade-off between volume and gross?

The answer is that, yes, there typically is a trade-off between volume and gross in used vehicles, just as there typically is in prudent investing. The difference for dealers, however, is that we're now able to capture gross without sacrificing volume—because we now understand the vehicles that can command the gross and investment return they deserve and, better still, we know how to treat them properly from Day 1.

You see, through all the work from Chris Stutsman and the data science team, we now know there are some vehicles for which there is little to no correlation between how they're priced and how quickly they move. We also know there are many other vehicles where there's a small degree of sensitivity or correlation between how they're priced and how quickly they move. That's right. There literally are cars where it doesn't matter how high you price them. They will still move fast. We now know how to identify these vehicles and we know why they're so special.

These vehicles are your Platinum and Gold vehicles. What makes these vehicles so special? Well, beyond the fact that these are vehicles you were able to acquire for a low Cost to Market, they have a low Market Days Supply and they are high volume movers in your market, there are other factors at work.

The other factors often don't get enough attention or credit. They relate to your salespeople.

Consider the days when you might have sold used vehicles. When you looked at the inventory you were charged to sell, what did you see? If you're like most sales associates in dealerships, you saw varying levels of commissionable gross opportunity in the cars you had in stock. Put another way, you were probably more excited to sell the cars with higher gross opportunity. This reality is a reason why some cars sell fast and some sell slowly.

Anyone who has sold used vehicles knows this to be true. We've all walked people to cars they didn't come in to see, and walked people around vehicles that brought them to your store. Why did we do that? We did it to optimize our commissionable gross opportunity.

With the Platinum and Gold vehicles, in particular, their ability to sell quickly, no matter how high we price them, also owes at least in part to your salespeople following the money. Haven't we all seen situations where a trade comes in, the plates haven't been removed, and salespeople are on the phone calling customers? We know this is true. It happens because your salespeople have a list of people who asked to call them first when a car like the one you just took into your inventory becomes available.

Now, why would customers ask your salespeople for this preferential treatment? The answer is because the cars they seek are the ones that are popular in the market, with high demand and short supply. And guess what? You're lucky enough to have just taken one into your inventory. Even better, your salesperson is motivated to sell the vehicle and make a good gross because you own it cheap. These factors are, by definition, what makes these Platinum and Gold vehicles.

Some of you may be thinking: But wait, I understand why salespeople are excited to sell Platinum and Gold vehicles, but where's their incentive to sell the Bronze and Silver vehicles, where there's little gross opportunity? It's a fair question. The answer, I believe, is because these vehicles, which you priced to move, will have motivated buyers who will effectively walk your salespeople to the vehicles they want to purchase. But it must be stated that this dynamic will not happen if your Bronze and Silver vehicle investments haven't been priced to move.

So, while we're selling Silver and Bronze cars at a higher rate of speed, we're going to take the Platinum and Gold cars and price them up. Way up, because now we understand there's little sensitivity or correlation between how we price them and how quickly they move.

Sometimes dealers who adopt an investment-minded strategy and the data science-driven system that supports it resist pricing Platinum and Gold vehicles properly. They often don't think they can ask for all the gross profit the data science is telling them a vehicle can command.

In response, I'll tell them that if you truly have a Platinum vehicle, put it on the market and ask $1 million, and watch how fast it sells. Obviously, customers aren't going to pay you $1 million. But they'll blow up your phone and break down your door. Customers will say, "this must be a joke" or "let's get real." The vehicle will sell and we all know that the higher we start with the price of a vehicle the more we make in the end.

It's also true that if you put a Platinum and Gold car on the internet without a price it will sell quickly. To be sure, our industry has done a good job convincing us that if you put a vehicle on the internet without a price it won't sell. But we now know this blanket statement isn't true. You'll still get action on these vehicles because they are the ones in high demand and short supply—the ones customers are searching to buy.

As I work with dealers who have adopted prudent investment management in used vehicles, I'm struck by the irony that, for years, I argued with dealers about lowering the price of their vehicles to sell them quickly. And today, I am spending significant time trying to convince them to raise their prices on Platinum and Gold and they argue with me. Why wouldn't you want to raise the price? The first response goes like this, "If I do that, I won't get any eyeballs or VDPs [vehicle details pages]." I'll respond by saying a lack of eyeballs and VDPs doesn't seem to bother you on the Silver and Bronze cars you've overpriced to the market.

After a chuckle, I'll reiterate the reality for Platinum and Gold vehicles. That is, you don't want to get eyeballs and VDPs on these vehicles because the only way to do that is by lowering your price. You don't need to do that on Platinum and Gold cars because customers are on the hunt for them. Customers will find and engage you on these vehicles no matter how you price them.

In the end, the good news that comes from adopting an investment value-based strategy for managing your used vehicle investments, and apply prudent investment management principles across the vehicles in your inventory portfolio, far outshines any bad news or difficulty you'll likely encounter as you adopt this new strategy-driven method of used vehicle investment management. You're going to sell more Silver and Bronze vehicles and you're going to make a lot more money on your Platinum and Gold vehicles, which will require more patience because these vehicles tend to move no matter what.

Even better, the faster pace of Silver and Bronze vehicle investment sales, and the ongoing gross-generating Platinum and Gold vehicle investment sales, will get consistently better over time. How? The data science behind the proper pricing recommendations for the mix of high-, medium-, and low-risk assets you own gets better over time the more you apply and trust it.

I would also add the good news that comes from adopting the principles of prudent investing, and an investment value-based strategy for managing used vehicles isn't limited to the outcomes that follow proper pricing of your Platinum, Gold, Silver, and Bronze investments. In fact, the benefits of shifting to an investment value-based strategy extend to the way you acquire, appraise, *and* price used vehicles.

We dive into how you can implement an investment value-based strategy and bring the good news to your dealership in subsequent chapters. First, though, let's take a moment to understand how the new investment-minded strategy differs from the more traditional turn-and-earn strategy that's defined many used vehicle departments for nearly past nearly 20 years, and why it makes rational sense to make the strategic shift sooner rather than later.

PART III

INTEGRATING STRATEGY INTO A DECISION-MAKING SYSTEM

CHAPTER 12

HOW INVESTMENT-MINDED MANAGEMENT TESTS TRADITIONAL THINKING

Let's step back for just a moment and consider how we've managed used vehicles for much of the past 20 years.

With the turn and earn or Velocity approach, we managed all cars the same. We priced them all as competitively as we could, to sell them all as quickly as we could. We operated with the understanding that the more you could turn your vehicles, the better. All in all, it was effectively a one-size-fits all approach.

Let's contrast that approach to where we are today. We now understand that every single vehicle has its own unique profile of risk and opportunity. Thanks to data science and discovery, we can develop the profile through the proper weighting of each vehicle's Cost to Market, Market Days Supply, and retail sales volume.

Once we accept that every vehicle has its own unique profile of risk and opportunity, doesn't it make rational sense to manage each vehicle in a way that gives it the opportunity to achieve its greatest investment return potential, whether it's large or small? The only way this doesn't make sense is if you believe that all cars are the same.

Let's consider what I think we can all agree to be good parenting. What does it mean to be a good parent? Does it mean treating all of your kids exactly the same and giving them all the same things? I don't think so. To me, good parenting means that you recognize each child is different. Each child has inherent strengths and weaknesses. As good parents, we hopefully have the ability to give each child what they need to achieve their greatest opportunity, whether it's large or small.

The essence of good parenting applies to used vehicles, especially now that we have the ability, through data science, to perceive and understand each vehicle's unique profile of risk and opportunity. With this understanding, doesn't it just make sense to manage each used vehicle in a manner designed to achieve its greatest opportunity?

It seems implausible to me that this approach cannot be right. It's just rational—unless you believe that all vehicles are the same.

This newly understood need to begin treating each used vehicle in accord with its own unique profile of risk and opportunity is the reason I call the new investment-minded approach to managing used vehicles Variable Management. It's a little unfortunate that the term "variable" has a different meaning in the car business, but Variable Management is the right term to describe the philosophy behind an investment-minded used vehicle management strategy that requires taking a different approach to each used vehicle, based on its profile of investment risk and potential.

But getting past the belief that every vehicle is the same, and you should treat them all the same way as you price them, is only one of the ways that the Variable Management strategy, and the system and playbook we've established to support it, tests the traditional Velocity or turn and earn approach to retailing used vehicles.

Let's have a look.

CHAPTER 13

RETHINKING INVENTORY "AGE" MANAGEMENT

Ever since I've been in the car business, almost every dealer I know, including me, had an age policy for our used vehicle inventory. We set ours for 60 days. When a vehicle reached that threshold as a retail unit, we wholesaled it and took our lumps.

But as the industry becomes more attuned to the investment-minded Variable Management strategy, I would like nothing better than for all of us to stop referring to these policies as "age" policies.

The first reason I call for this change in our vernacular may seem trite. I only want to change a word.

Well, sometimes words matter. Sometimes words matter a lot. I believe this is a context where words matter a lot.

As an industry, we should stop calling it an age policy. We're not museum curators. We're salespeople. We're not here to age cars. We're here to turn cars.

That's why I believe we should stop using the term age policy in favor of calling it a turn policy. Why? Because I believe that calling it a turn policy more directly conveys our mission to our people—we're here to turn vehicles.

The second reason I believe we should call them turn policies rather than age policies is far more fundamental than a word change.

To be clear, I do believe and always will believe that dealers should have a policy, whether you want to call it age or turn. But what I absolutely no longer believe, because I now know better thanks to all the data science work, is that it makes no sense to have the same policy for every vehicle—whether it's 30, 45, 60, or 90 days or some other number.

Why? Well, let's think about it. An age or turn policy that you apply to every vehicle implicitly assumes that every vehicle is the same in terms of its potential and risk. Yet we now know that's not true, and you would have to believe that's true to support a policy by which every used vehicle gets the same chance. It just isn't rational.

A far more rational and sensible approach would be what I call a "variable turn policy." A variable turn policy is a fundamental part of the investment-minded Variable Management strategy. It recognizes that some cars with great potential should be given the opportunity to achieve that great potential with a high gross price. If necessary, we should be prepared to be more patient with these vehicles to enable them to achieve their optimal investment return. On the other hand, there are vehicles that hold significant risk. Consequently, we should show those vehicles the greatest urgency and price them to move more quickly. How can this approach not be a more rational way to manage our used vehicle investments, unless you believe every vehicle holds the same potential?

Given our new understanding about each vehicle's unique potential, I believe the time has arrived to do away with static age policies that treat every vehicle the same. Instead, we must usher in an era where dealers manage their used vehicle investments in a more variable manner. Why? Again, it's because this variable turn approach recognizes the reality that every single used vehicle is different, and every single used vehicle holds its own unique profile of risk and opportunity, and therefore it's just rational to treat your used vehicle investments in a variable manner.

What does the variable turn policy look like in practice? If it were my store, it would look something like Table 13.1.

For my best cars—the ones I own for the best money, with the lowest Market Days Supply and highest retail volume—I'll price them high and give them the opportunity to achieve the large gross they are capable of producing. If necessary, I'll give these vehicles—my Platinum investments—an average of 50 days to turn. Would

Table 13.1. Variable Management done right

	Percentage of vehicles	Average Price to Market	Average Cost to Market	Average days in inventory	Average days to sell
Platinum	14%	102%	74%	48	50
Gold	23%	100%	84%	36	40
Silver	25%	98%	89%	28	30
Bronze	27%	96%	95%	20	20

anyone be offended to have their best vehicles turn for the biggest grosses in an average of 50 days? I don't think so.

Next, with my Gold vehicle investments, I want them to turn in an average of 40 days. I'll look to turn my Silver vehicle investments in 30 days. Then, with my Bronze vehicles, which represent the biggest risk because of a high Cost to Market, high Market Days Supply, and low retail sales volume, I want them to move in an average of 20 days to maximize whatever gross profit or return on investment (ROI) potential they hold quickly, before it fades because of depreciation and other market factors.

Not surprisingly, the variable turn approach exactly reflects how prudent investors manage portfolios with a diverse mix of assets with varying degrees of risk and opportunity.

We discuss the specifics of how dealers can implement the variable turn policy as we address how the investment-minded Variable Management strategy extends to used vehicle pricing in an upcoming chapter.

Before we go there, though, it's important for everyone to understand how and why the investment-based Variable Management strategy, and the playbook we created to support it, goes beyond just pricing vehicles.

Let's take a look.

CHAPTER 14

FOUNDATIONAL PRINCIPLES OF THE VARIABLE MANAGEMENT PLAYBOOK

Every dealer understands that there are many things that influence the outcome and performance of the used vehicle department.

But I would submit that the three areas of used vehicle operations that have the greatest impact on the outcome and performance of a used vehicle department consist of the Big Three—vehicle acquisition, appraising, and pricing. I would also submit that none of these mission-critical areas of used vehicle operations, and the distinct processes associated with each, currently account for the fact that, as we now understand, every used vehicle holds its own unique profile of investment risk and opportunity.

That's one of the foundational principles behind the playbook we've developed to help dealers implement an investment-minded

Variable Management strategy for managing used vehicles. If our goal is to help dealers become more prudent managers of their used vehicle investments, the playbook needs to cover the critical processes that ultimately determine whether a used vehicle investment can achieve its greatest potential.

Historically, I think most dealers would agree that the people and processes that drive vehicle acquisition, appraising, and pricing often do not work in harmony. If the used vehicle department is like a stool that stands on the three mission-critical legs of the Big Three, the stool is often out of balance. How many times have we acquired the wrong car, paid too much for a vehicle, or priced a vehicle incorrectly?

The new playbook we've created to support the investment-minded Variable Management strategy aims to end such imbalances by helping dealers bring five operational principles to life across vehicle acquisition, appraising, and pricing:

1. *Establish a strategy.* The overarching principle behind the Variable Management strategy and playbook is that we are not just managing merchandise, we are managing a portfolio of unique, individual used vehicle investments. Therefore, our end goal must be to optimize the net profit or ROI potential inherent in each vehicle.

2. *Clearly communicate the strategy.* I would submit that some of the imbalances across the Big Three of used vehicle operations owes to the fact that our people are often unaware of our strategy, or they're unsure of how they should execute it.

3. *Connect your strategy to day-to-day decisions and process.* If we want the Big Three to operate in sync with each other, our people will need strategy-connected guidance to make the right decisions and do the right things.

4. *Measure process execution and performance.* The key here is each team member's ability to make decisions and perform tasks in accord with your strategic objectives.

5. *Manage your people, performance, and process.* It doesn't matter how well you might measure an employee's performance if you aren't proactively managing it to achieve your desired outcomes.

Readers who have studied business management will recognize the principles that underlie the Variable Management strategy and the playbook that supports it. They reflect the characteristics of well-run, successful long-term businesses. Some readers may also recognize the principles from their own business plans, and they may also appreciate how, despite their best efforts, it's difficult to operate with each of the five principles in sync at all times.

Part of dealers' inability to consistently operate their used vehicle departments in accord with these principles owes, at least in part, to the nature of the technology and tools they use to run their businesses. In many instances, the tools are more task-oriented. Their functionality isn't necessarily tied to a dealer's strategic objectives. They typically don't give employees, who are charged with making decisions and performing tasks in line with a dealer's strategy, the kind of in-the-moment decisioning they need to stay on strategy. As a result, the tools are often lacking in their ability to measure and manage performance in a way that helps dealers understand each employee's ability to make decisions and perform in a way that supports the dealer's strategic objectives.

The vAuto team and I recognized these deficiencies. We understood that if we are to find success helping dealers implement an investment-minded strategy in used vehicles, and adopt the new Variable Management playbook, we'd need to build a system that makes all this possible.

That's exactly what we've done. Let's have a look.

CHAPTER 15

SHAPING A SYSTEM TO BRING INVESTMENT-MINDED MANAGEMENT TO YOUR BIG THREE

One of the advantages the vAuto team and I had in our favor as we began to sketch out a system that would support the new investment-minded Variable Management strategy and playbook came from our history developing and innovating vAuto's Provision system.

Years ago, we built the Provision system to support the turn-and-earn, or Velocity-based, strategy of inventory management. The system served up the live market data and metrics dealers and their teams needed to make decisions consistent with whatever form of the turn-and-earn or Velocity strategy a dealer favored. As Provision users know, the system also has a rich library of reports that help you keep track of your cars, the state of your inventory and the performance of your team as they performed the tasks within the processes that drive the Big Three—vehicle acquisition, appraising, and pricing.

As we set out to build a system that would support the new investment-minded Variable Management strategy and playbook, we knew we needed to go farther and further than we'd ever gone with Provision to help dealers truly become the prudent managers of used vehicle investments we knew they would need to be.

For example, while the Provision system was purpose-built to support the Velocity strategy, the system itself did not really allow a dealer to calibrate the vehicle acquisition, appraising, or pricing tools to reflect their preferred form of the Velocity strategy. In other words, the Provision system didn't necessarily guide users to the optimal outcome for any used vehicle. Rather, the system put the onus on individuals who used it to decide how they should behave and think as they acquired, appraised, and priced vehicles. In turn, the system didn't make it super-easy for dealers and managers to assess the extent to which their teams made decisions and performed process-oriented tasks in line with the dealer's preferred strategy.

To be clear, I'm not knocking the Provision system. It still stands as the industry's best used vehicle inventory management solution for dealers who have not yet come to understand what the data science now tells us to be true: That every used vehicle has its own unique profile of investment risk and opportunity, and every used vehicle should be given the opportunity to achieve its optimal ROI potential, however large or small it might be.

Our learnings from all the years of building and innovating Provision helped us go to another level as we shaped a system that would support the new investment-minded Variable Management strategy and playbook across vehicle acquisition, appraising, and pricing. As we whiteboarded the system, we drew from the principles that serve as the foundation for the Variable Management strategy and playbook, as well as our experience working with Provision dealers.

First, we knew the system must give dealers the flexibility to calibrate the system to support their preferred investment strategy. Our data science work affirmed that just as the investment potential of every vehicle is different, the strategic goals of any dealer's used vehicle department are different. Some dealers like to maximize volume. Some go for gross. Some prefer a balance between the two. As we thought through these realities, we knew a software system must allow a dealer to upload and dial in the investment strategy that helps them meet their distinct goals.

Second, we recognized that the dealer's chosen investment strategy must filter across and through all dealership-based decisions and related processes that have a hand in shaping each used vehicle's investment or ROI potential (i.e., the Big Three) and guide individuals to the most investment-optimal decision, in the moment, with every vehicle. In this way, the new system goes much farther than Provision, which informs but doesn't guide decision-making. The data-science-based guidance the system provides helps mitigate the tug of human nature and individual biases and beliefs that result in suboptimal decisions that, all too often, don't reflect a dealer's preferred strategy.

Third, we understood that if the end game is to help dealers truly optimize each vehicle's ROI in accord with their investment strategy, we needed a way to give dealers visibility into the day-to-day decision-making that they previously didn't have. If you can't see something, you can't measure its effectiveness. If you can't measure effectiveness, you can't really coach or manage anyone to make better decisions and achieve better outcomes. As we built a software system to support strategy-tied decision-making across vehicle acquisition, appraising, and pricing, we created an industry-first—rich, robust displays of in-the-moment decision-making so dealers and managers can see, measure, and manage an individual's ability to make strategy-guided decisions, and coach or course-correct when appropriate.

While building the system, we also realized we'd need a name. We landed on ProfitTime GPS as the name for the new solution. We chose ProfitTime because it speaks to what we now understand to bc thc variablc naturc of the investment risk and opportunity profile each vehicle possesses. The name's a nod to the fact that the time to make profit on any specific vehicle is different than the vehicle next to it.

The "GPS" part of the system's name stands for Global Profitability System. We borrowed "GPS" from the global positioning systems we now all depend on for driving. Like the GPS in a car, ProfitTime GPS guides dealers and their teams to optimally manage each vehicle's profit or ROI potential across the Big Three of acquisition, appraising, and pricing. Also, like the in-vehicle and phone-based GPS tools we all use, ProfitTime GPS draws from data science to continually assesses and refine guidance on the most efficient and optimal way of achieving each vehicle's optimal ROI outcome as market conditions change. The end goal for ProfitTime

GPS is to help dealers and their teams arrive at the right ROI-minded destination with every vehicle, based on the dealer's overall investment strategy objective.

I'm excited to detail how ProfitTime GPS supports the Variable Management strategy and playbook to help dealers manage their used vehicles as investments, helping them achieve a higher level of inventory, process, and strategy optimization across the entirety of their used vehicle operations.

Before we go there, though, it's important to understand why the time has arrived for this important transition to the data-science-driven, investment-minded Variable Management strategy and the ProfitTime GPS system that supports it.

CHAPTER 16

EVOLUTION OF DATA-SCIENCE-DRIVEN AND INVESTMENT-MINDED DECISION-MAKING

As I've seen dealers and managers adopt ProfitTime GPS to execute the investment-minded Variable Management strategy it supports, it's clear that some of the data science– and investment-oriented principles and process changes that the strategy requires feel foreign, difficult to sustain, and in some cases, not even worth the effort to give them an honest college try.

There are many factors that give rise to such discomfort and outright resistance. Each is worth exploring in greater detail. I do that in upcoming chapters.

For now, though, I think it's important for everyone to understand that the shift to managing each used vehicle investment to achieve its optimal ROI outcome, and relying on data-science-driven insights and recommendations to get there, is nothing new in the broader world of business. In fact, in multiple industries, the use of data science to achieve ROI-positive outcomes from all sorts of retail investments is now par for the course. It is, in fact, how business gets done.

The problem for dealers and our industry, it seems, is that we're one of the last to arrive at this party. We don't know anyone. The party feels different. The drinks and food they're serving don't seem appealing. Should we just turn around and go home?

Unfortunately, given the way businesses everywhere have adopted data-science-based solutions to achieve better outcomes for their bottom lines, I believe it will only be a matter of time before dealers won't have the option to turn around and go home. They may well be out of business as competitors, who are less resistant to new ways of thinking and operating, gain greater advantage.

There's no better case study for this reality than the world of investing.

Prior to 1975, I think it's fair to say that the bulk of investment decisions on behalf of individual and institutional investors were made by an individual—a broker, a financial advisor, or a stock picker.

Such individuals would at least advise, if not decide, where their clients should invest their money. The guidance and decision-making often flowed from the individual's experience, expertise, and track record.

In this era, it wasn't uncommon for a single individual to have the equivalent of a "hot hand," where they seemed to have the ability to amass a track record of profit-positive investment decisions compared to losses. Many of these individuals became quite rich and successful.

But in early 1970s, all this changed. Top economists had questioned whether any one individual's decision-making could be superior to a more balanced, data-indexed style of investing—where investment portfolios were built on a cross-section of different types of investments, based on objective measures of their past performance and future performance projections, rather than someone's experience and judgment.

One of the top economists, Robert Samuelson, issued a challenge for someone to turn this idea for a data-driven index fund into a reality—ultimately to disprove the notion that a single individual could outperform the data-driven decision-making. In 1975, Jack Bogle heeded the challenge and started the world's first index fund, Vanguard Group.

We should all be aware of how this story has turned out. Vanguard is the number-one index fund in the world, a preferred choice for millions of people and institutions looking to optimize the ROI from their financial investments.

Data-science-driven decision-making has also found an essential home in other industries—even some that are closely tied to the car business. Just ask your F&I manager how often they can get a rep from your captive or third-party finance office on the horn to "work a deal" with a customer with an unfortunate credit history that doesn't fit the company's approval algorithms.

Doctors. Farmers. Restaurant owners. They're all using data science in one form or another to make their businesses more investment-efficient and profitable.

My point here is to showcase where the winds of data science and new technologies are blowing. Over time, dealers will face the choice of adopting the technology and tools that enable data-science-driven decision-making or continue to resist. And, as I note above, sooner or later, there will be no choice.

Beyond dealers, who will ultimately decide the future course of their used vehicle business, the individuals who sit most squarely at the intersection of emerging data-science-driven decision-making and expertise/experience-driven decision-making are the used vehicle managers at individual dealerships. They will be the ones most put to the test by the new Variable Management strategy for managing used vehicle investments to achieve optimal ROI.

It's my hope that the next chapter offers some perspective to help today's used vehicle managers retain command of their destiny in the years ahead and dealers do their part to sustain the captain's longevity and success.

CHAPTER 17

HOW THE ROLE OF YOUR USED VEHICLE MANAGER IS CHANGING

If we go back to the earliest days of the used car business, when dealers decided that the business had grown to sufficient size that they needed to put someone in charge of a fledgling used vehicle department, there were two principal rules that guided who might get this important job.

Rule 1: The individual must have used vehicle experience. I suspect the earliest dealers did what dealers do today to find the person they'll put in charge of the used vehicle department. They'll find someone who's got a decent track record of selling used vehicles, who understands the used vehicles that sell the best for a store and market, who knows how to appraise and price vehicles and, to a lesser extent, who knows how to lead and manage their sales and support teams.

Rule 2: The used vehicle manager knows best. Given the emphasis on past experience, dealers, who often have more affinity with their new vehicle departments, tend to give used vehicle managers a fair amount of latitude to make decisions. That's why they are effectively the ones who determine and guide how the used vehicle department performs month after month. They ultimately answer to a higher authority, but the day-to-day decisions are made, and largely go unchecked, with a shared understanding that the used vehicle manager knows best.

I would submit that as dealers ask their used vehicle managers to become more prudent managers of their used vehicle investments, each of these rules, and the culture of confidence and decision-making latitude they create, will be put to the test.

But let me make it clear. Neither of these rules goes away. Rather, they simply evolve to slightly different forms as decision-making follows the data-science-driven insights that lead to optimal ROI outcomes for each vehicle. In fact, a used vehicle manager's experience and expertise matters *more than ever* in today's data-science-driven business. Why? Because individual used vehicle managers not only become the chief stewards of a dealer's investment strategy. They, like prudent investment managers, become the ultimate arbiters of deciding if the data science is telling them the whole story about the asset they are considering for their inventory portfolios.

As I note in the last chapter, while today's top investment managers rely on data science and technology to assess and manage investments, they ultimately determine if the data-science-driven assessment of each asset's potential opportunity and risk squares up with the reality on the ground. The same is true for used vehicle managers. For example, the data science behind the ProfitTime

GPS system may determine a vehicle's a top-tier investment, a Platinum vehicle, and ranks the highest on the system's 1–12 investment score scale.

But it's the used vehicle manager who decides if the vehicle, which might be a pink Jeep Wrangler that's loaded with accessories or has a bad smell, may not play as a Platinum vehicle, or should be priced as a Platinum vehicle, in a local market. Today's data science is good, but it can't yet catch every detail, about every vehicle, that might have a significant impact on its investment opportunity and risk profile. The used vehicle manager, who's able to put eyes, ears, and a nose on every vehicle, *can* assess these important characteristics and account for them as they manage the investment. In the case of a Platinum Jeep Wrangler, the manager might decide the vehicle is more properly managed as a low-Gold or high-Silver investment.

Similarly, a used vehicle manager's decision-making latitude doesn't fundamentally change. To be sure, while the investment-minded Variable Management strategy that ProfitTime GPS supports establishes strategic guidelines to help dealers achieve their investment objectives across acquisition, appraising, and pricing, the used vehicle manager still has plenty of decision-making room to operate the department as they see best. I would add that an individual used vehicle manager's comfort level with the strategic boundaries often depend, to a great extent, on how the dealer establishes them. In the best case, the used vehicle manager has a seat at the table—with the dealer—to at least inform, if not shape, the respective acquisition, appraising and pricing strategies that will define the used vehicle department's investment and ROI objectives.

To the extent that such changes make a used vehicle manager uncomfortable, I would point to other professions where other individuals, who are in charge of making mission-critical decisions, now operate differently, in sync with data-science-driven insights and recommendations, until situations arrive where their expertise and judgment should carry the day.

Take commercial airplane pilots, for example. The only times today's pilots are truly in control, and flying the plane manually, occurs on take-offs and landings. Otherwise, the planes largely fly based on data science and machine learning that's built into the automated flight control systems—unless and until the pilot senses something's off and needs to step in.

It's a similar situation for the captains of commercial cargo ships. More and more, the ships sail on their own, powered by sophisticated data-science-enabled navigation and control systems, until something happens, like entering into a harbor or confronting high waves and wind, that requires their intervention and oversight.

I suspect some airline pilots and ship captains resisted the introduction of data-science-driven insights into their decision-making and workflows. They probably said, "No thank you," and opted to fly planes and sail ships that don't operate with the data-science-enabled technologies and tools. Others, however, embraced the inevitable—and they're the ones flying the planes and sailing the ships the future will bring.

The same situation applies to dealers and used vehicle managers now that data-science-enabled strategies and decision-making have arrived in the car business. My hope is that the subsequent sections of the book help everyone see how they can, in fact, find even greater success as they use the data-science-driven system like ProfitTime GPS to become the prudent managers of used vehicle investments the market will ask and require them to be.

We start the discussion by examining how dealers can establish the vehicle acquisition strategy that helps shape their used vehicle investment portfolios.

PART IV

USING THE SYSTEM TO EXECUTE YOUR ACQUISITION STRATEGY

CHAPTER 18

UNPACKING A PERSISTENT STRATEGIC VEHICLE ACQUISITION DEFICIENCY

If we view most dealers' used vehicle inventories as investment portfolios, they often suggest that dealers aren't following, or even considering, the common strategic principles that prudent investment managers follow as they create and manage investment portfolios for their clients.

One of the first things investment managers do when they take on a new client is talk strategy. They sit down with the clients and discuss their investment objectives: When do you want to retire? What kind of income level do you expect to need for your retirement? What level of risk and reward are you willing to undertake as you invest your money? How much money are you looking to invest? From there, investment managers will determine the right number and mix of investment assets that will go into a client's portfolio to meet the agreed-on objectives.

But such conversations rarely happen in dealerships between dealers and the individuals, often used vehicle directors or managers, who hold the responsibility for acquiring the assets or vehicles that will make up the dealer's inventory portfolio from one month to the next. The evidence of this lack of strategy-based inventory investment portfolio development tends to manifest month after month. Consider how often dealers:

1. *Realize they don't have enough cars.* Maybe you had the good fortune of selling more than you expected in a prior month. Maybe your acquisition team fell behind. Whatever the case, your inventory portfolio isn't where it should be. A typical response to inventory shortfalls is someone goes out to "get some cars."

2. *Realize you have too many cars.* It seems like this predicament happens every year around May or June—you stocked up for the spring selling season and sales didn't pan out. Now, you've got more cars than you need, and your inventory portfolio's out of balance.

3. *Your mix isn't right.* I consider this problem to be the equivalent of a kind of cancer that causes damage but isn't discernible unless you test for it. For years, vAuto Performance Managers and I coached dealers on the best way to align their mix to what's selling in the market. Unfortunately, the coaching often falls on deaf ears or it's

forgotten as one month moves to the next—usually giving way to the judgment of someone who knows best, plays to their preferences and may not be capable of keeping up with the makes, models, and trim lines that matter most in a market.

As the vAuto team and I developed a system that would help dealers adopt an investment value-based approach to managing used vehicles, we recognized that the system must address the typical absence of a vehicle acquisition strategy, and give dealers and their management team a means to always maintain the right number of used vehicle assets in a dealership's inventory portfolio. The next chapter highlights how the system provides these first-ever capabilities and how they can mitigate the circumstances that lead to inventory shortfalls, oversupply or a suboptimal mix of used vehicle investments.

CHAPTER 19

A STRATEGIC, MARKET-BASED METHOD TO THE RIGHT NUMBER AND MIX IN YOUR INVENTORY PORTFOLIO

Besides ensuring that your inventory portfolio consistently reflects the right number and mix of vehicles for your dealership and market, a vehicle acquisition strategy also helps you establish a critical consideration that every prudent investment manager accounts for as they evaluate adding an investment to a client's portfolio—how much does your portfolio need the additional asset?

Think about it: If your acquisition team isn't consistently working to create an inventory portfolio that reflects the right number and mix of vehicles, is it possible for them to always know, when they're considering acquiring a vehicle, how much you need the vehicle? And wouldn't you be better off if they were aware of your relative level of "need" with every potential acquisition to know if they should step up, back, or away from it as a potential investment?

These are the fundamental questions the acquisition system inside ProfitTime GPS answers, at all times, for every dealer. The system's foundation is each dealer's vehicle acquisition strategy, which helps dealers and managers collaboratively base their acquisition strategy on their goals to drive volume, gross, or a balance of both for their used vehicle departments. Here's a quick look at the elements the strategy-based acquisition system enables to help dealers establish what the right number and mix of vehicles should be, and assure that their acquisition team is always aware of how much your inventory portfolio needs a vehicle as they're buying and bringing in vehicles.

Your annualized sales objective spread out across every month. The system goes beyond the typical calculations dealers or managers might use to forecast their annual sales objective at the beginning of a year. In my experience, dealers do this by assessing last year's total sales and dividing it by 12. Some might take a second step and project each prospective month's volume objective based on how they did in the same month the previous year. The system incorporates a wider range of past monthly performance data, seasonal market conditions and other factors to calculate a more market-based and realistic sales objective each month.

A dynamic, market-driven basis for monthly stocking levels. Once the system establishes your monthly sales objectives, it forecasts the number of vehicles you need to stock, accounting for the amount of time it takes you to get vehicles reconditioned and retail-ready. Most dealers and managers falter with this important consideration: They either don't have an accurate or objective read on the number of days it takes to get vehicles retail-ready, or their stocking objectives don't take reconditioning time into account. Our new system takes any reconditioning inefficiencies into account, helping you see, and potentially solve, how the delays affect the inventory you need to stock every month.

A market-driven view of the vehicle segments, types, and price points you should stock. Using past dealership performance and market data, the system helps dealers and managers establish the target days supply and monthly sales they expect to achieve across individual vehicle segments, types, and price points. At this stage, the system helps dealers identify the specific inventory pockets where they customarily are too light or too heavy. It also cross-checks these segments against market sales data to identify the specific vehicles, by brand and segment, that a dealer should be stocking.

A forecast of where you'll acquire your vehicles. This step is almost entirely overlooked by dealers and managers. Why? It's because most don't keep track of the segments and types of vehicles they typically acquire by distinct sourcing channels. They might know, for example, that they take in four or five trades with every 10 new or used vehicles they sell. They might also know how many auction vehicles they typically acquire every month. But for other sourcing channels that have become critically important, dealers often guesstimate what they're getting, if they're mining these channels at all.

The new system corrects this problem by automatically assigning a vehicle to its sourcing channel, to give dealers a baseline understanding of the number, type, and average investment value of vehicles they acquire in each channel. Next, it forecasts the number of vehicles dealers can expect to take in from each channel to achieve their monthly stocking objective. Even better, if a dealer intends to grow sales volume in a given year, the system helps them identify the specific channels where they can most likely acquire the additional inventory they'll need to meet their objective. In many cases, the system also effectively reveals ways for dealers to optimize inventory acquisitions from channels they haven't fully tapped.

Stocking objectives for individual buyers. Once the system has established the number of vehicles needed each month by sourcing channel, it distributes the work to individual buyers by giving them channel-specific stocking objectives. The idea, of course, is to give buyers a clearer sense of the number and types of vehicles they will be expected to acquire in distinct sourcing channels. In this way, the system better connects buyers to the inventory the used vehicle department truly needs in every channel. I would add that this aspect of establishing your inventory stocking strategy often proves revealing to dealers and managers. It tends to reveal surface buyer performance and channel-specific process improvement opportunities.

You may be thinking: "This system seems and sounds too complicated and time-consuming for me to figure out."

But therein lies the beauty of the system. From our experience working with dealers and their managers to configure the right mix and number of vehicles for their inventory portfolios, we understand dealers and managers may not have the brainpower and time to figure out all the complexities and sophistication that must go into developing a sound market- and needs-based vehicle acquisition strategy. That's why we built the new system effectively to do all the complicated calculations and work for you. My directive to the development team was very clear: While this system is very sophisticated, it can't be that way for the dealers, managers, and others who use it. I'm proud to say they listened, and the end result is a super-easy user experience.

Some readers may also be thinking: "I can see how this system will help me maintain the right number and mix of vehicles, and make sure we're acquiring the cars we need. But how on God's green earth will we get the cars?"

It's a fair question. To some extent, we remain in a supply-constrained used vehicle market that'll be with us for some time. But this is precisely the reason our new system connects to another innovation inside ProfitTime GPS, called Global Search, which shows you where the vehicles our stocking system says you need are available across every sourcing channel. It's another innovation that we've built to simplify life for your buyers and help them efficiently meet the monthly stocking objectives the system establishes for them.

Global Search has an awful lot of inventory sourcing power. Let's take a moment to go under the Global Search hood to help you see that getting the inventory you need to maintain your vehicle acquisition strategy and consistently carrying the proper number and mix of inventory isn't as difficult as it used to be.

CHAPTER 20

A MORE CONNECTED, EFFICIENT WAY TO ACQUIRE INVENTORY YOU NEED

One of the least glamorous and most critically important jobs in any dealership rests with the person who's in charge of acquiring used vehicle inventory. If this person isn't doing a good, if not great, job of finding and buying the right number and mix of inventory, the bad, suboptimal things that happen in the used vehicle department, which we've discussed in preceding chapters, extend to the entire dealership.

For example, if your used vehicle inventory number and mix isn't right, your ability to step up, or step back, from trade-ins hurts your new vehicle department. In turn, your F&I office sees fewer customers, or they arrive there less able to say yes to additional products. Similarly, your service department can suffer, dealing with a never-steady incoming supply of reconditioning work that causes delays and disruption.

Unfortunately, the COVID-19 pandemic and the shake-up it created in new and used vehicle supply/demand dynamics has made acquiring the right mix and number of vehicles for your inventory even more difficult. Trade-ins from new or used vehicle deals happen less frequently than they used to. The cost of auction vehicles remains historically high. We've entered an era where, in an ideal and optimal situation, used vehicle inventory must now be sourced from every possible channel—from your service drive to the street—to increase the chances that you can acquire the right number and mix of inventory, and buy them right to meet your used vehicle profit objectives.

This backdrop fueled the brainstorming sessions that led to the development of the Global Search solution in ProfitTime GPS. The vAuto development team and I understood that if we aspire to help dealers and their buyers, who now have specific, strategy-driven vehicle acquisition objectives, consistently acquire and maintain the right number and mix of used vehicles they need for their inventories and local markets, we needed to think beyond the walls of vAuto to develop a solution that would truly enable and power multichannel sourcing efficiency and success.

Our early development sessions quickly expanded to include teams from other Cox Automotive businesses, including Autotrader, Manheim, Kelley Blue Book Instant Cash Offer, VinSolutions, and Xtime. We understood this collective was essential if we were going to build a solution that would effectively serve up customers who own a vehicle they might want to sell or trade that fits a dealer's stocking strategy. We also struck a partnership with Vehicle Acquisition Network (VAN), to make sure our solution could extend beyond a dealer's current customer base, to local owners who also have a stocking strategy-aligned vehicle they are trying to sell.

We landed on a broad vision for Global Search that now achieves the following objectives.

Put all available and needed vehicles, across every channel, in one place. Dealers who have used vAuto's Stockwave solution have benefitted from an auction-focused version of this functionality. When Stockwave debuted, and to this day, it remains the only solution that aggregates all available auction vehicles—inside and outside the Manheim ecosystem—into a single platform. This solution also includes instant access to the tools buyers need to appraise and evaluate a vehicle to determine their max bid and/or a profit-acceptable purchase price.

Global Search builds on Stockwave's single-point connection to the wholesale market, using deep integrations with other Cox Automotive solutions to serve up cars and customers from a dealer's existing customer base (VinSolutions), service drive (Xtime), third-party classified sites and dealer websites (Autotrader, Kelley Blue Book Instant Cash Offer), and street purchases (VAN).

Make it "stupid-easy" to zero in on the best vehicles. From our experience with Manheim and Stockwave, we know that individual buyer workflow preferences must prevail. They need to be able to work the way they want to work, and look at the available vehicles in the manner and sequence they prefer. That's why Global Search offers what we consider to be the most robust set of user-set filters/search options to help buyers get to the cars they need faster than ever before, irrespective of the sourcing channel. The solution's set up this way to enable the channel-specific expertise that, over time, we believe every dealer will need to establish. That is, if you've got a team dedicated to acquiring vehicles from Kelley Blue Book Instant Cash Offer or your service drive, for example, you've now got a system that supports such specialization.

Serve up each vehicle's ROI potential. Global Search's connection to the deep data science behind ProfitTime GPS allows Global Search to serve up each vehicle's ROI potential as buyers appraise and evaluate each potential acquisition. Users can filter/search vehicles by their Platinum, Gold, Silver or Bronze designations, and understand how the investment value might change as they fully assess each vehicle's condition, factor in their cost expectations (i.e., buy fees/transportation if it's an auction unit). In the next chapter, we explore how bringing ROI-minded insights to the point of acquisition helps buyers know they're buying the right car for the right money, or at least they attempted to.

Give dealers and managers a holistic view of buyer performance. To date, even the best dealers are largely relegated to addressing situations where buyers either paid too much for a vehicle, or they bought the wrong car (i.e., it wasn't really needed or it fell too far outside a store's stocking strategy) until it's too late. This reality contributes to dealers' collective inability to consistently maintain the right number and mix of inventory. Global Search tackles this long-standing challenge by connecting more seamlessly to the appraisal tools inside ProfitTime GPS. This connection point now surfaces, in the moment, when a buyer's appraising a car in any channel, if a dealer or manager chooses, whether the buyer's landed on the right car and/or the right money.

All in all, the vAuto development team view Global Search as a significant step forward for dealers and used vehicle department managers. The level of oversight, and visibility into in-the-moment coaching/performance improvement opportunities, goes a long way to helping used vehicle departments consistently carry the right number and mix of inventory.

Now, let's explore Global Search's connections to ProfitTime GPS's appraisal system to help you understand how and why your buyers can be more "right" with the money they invest in each vehicle more often—and how you can finally tame the Wild, Wild West that appraising vehicles has become for dealers.

PART V

USING THE SYSTEM TO EXECUTE YOUR APPRAISAL STRATEGY

CHAPTER 21

A STRATEGIC PATH TO TAME THE WILD, WILD WEST OF APPRAISING VEHICLES

Once dealers and their managers establish an investment-minded strategy for acquiring vehicles, it's an absolute must for appraisers and buyers who will be acquiring the assets for your inventory portfolio to know how to land each vehicle on the right money.

Unfortunately, this is no easy task for any dealer.

Why? It's because our industry, and very few, if any dealers, have ever had the means to truly know what the right money for any vehicle should be at any moment in the market.

Now, I'm sure some dealers and managers may *think* they know what the right money should be for any vehicle at any moment. You may even take pride in the way you've coached and trained your appraisers and buyers to arrive at the right money for any vehicle in any situation.

But I would submit that the day-to-day realities of appraising vehicles, coupled with the beliefs and biases appraisers apply as they evaluate a vehicle's condition and determine its value, and a lack of robust appraiser performance management, have helped appraising become the last remaining Wild, Wild West in almost every dealership. In this current state, everyone effectively does their own thing. There's little, if any, shared understanding of what the right money for any vehicle should be. There's too little process consistency. Worst of all, there's a glaring absence of an overarching appraisal strategy to guide everyone to the right money and the most ROI-optimal decisions with every vehicle.

We can get a glimpse of how wild the state of appraising vehicles has become through the metrics some dealers use today to evaluate how well their appraisers and buyers are doing their jobs:

Acquisition Cost to Market: Of all the currently available appraiser performance metrics, this one comes closest to helping appraisers understand what the right money for a vehicle should be. As many readers know, the metric measures a vehicle's appraised value against prevailing retail prices for the same/similar units. Dealers often like to see some consistency across individual appraisers—say, a goal to bring in vehicles at Cost to Market percentages around 80 percent to 85 percent.

But here's the problem: If we accept and believe that each vehicle has its own profile of investment risk and opportunity, does a standard Cost to Market performance target for appraisers make any sense? It's a crude way to measure the right money for any vehicle and appraisers know it. That's why we tend to see acquisition Cost to Market averages vary by as much as 15 percent to 20 percent among appraisers—a disparity that means two appraisers often land $1,000 or more apart on the same $20,000 vehicle. Does such a gap suggest everyone knows what the right money should be for any vehicle?

Look to book: As most readers should know, this metric measures how many cars you take in compared to the total number you appraise. Generally speaking, our industry regards a roughly 50 percent look to book rate as good performance. But, across individual appraisers and individual sourcing channels, we often see double-digit differences—yet another sign that individual appraisers aren't operating from a standard, strategy-based playbook.

Default reconditioning estimates: If we really cared about putting the right money into every vehicle, you'd think we'd see more comprehensive and consistent assessments of each vehicle's condition and the costs needed to recondition a vehicle for retail sale. But here again, that's not what we see in the Wild, Wild West of appraising. An analysis of appraiser performance among vAuto dealers in the spring of 2024 revealed that almost 70 percent of dealers allow default reconditioning costs for more than 50 percent of the vehicles their teams appraise and acquire. If you break this group down further, 41 percent of the dealers use default reconditioning estimates more than 80 percent of the time. The data suggest a significant opportunity for dealers to move their teams closer to knowing how to arrive at the right money for each vehicle and to eliminate variances in the cost of goods sold for each used vehicle investment as vehicles move into and out of reconditioning.

As the vAuto teams and I developed the appraising system inside ProfitTime GPS, we realized that if we aspire to help dealers become more prudent managers of their used vehicle investments, we'd need to help them tame the Wild, Wild West of appraising. We established the following principles to shape how the system would help dealers achieve this outcome in unprecedented ways.

Give dealers the ability to create an appraisal strategy that establishes what the right money should be for any vehicle. The system allows dealers and top managers to establish an appraisal strategy that connects to their overall investment and ROI objectives. From there, the system takes the dealer's strategic investment objectives and couples it with a dealer's vehicle acquisition strategy and live market data to determine what the right money for any vehicle should be.

Give dealers the ability to automatically "call in the play" with every appraisal. This aspect of the appraisal system inside ProfitTime GPS does two things. First, it ensures that every appraiser, with every vehicle, has a clear understanding of what the right money should be at the moment of decision-making. The end goal is more investment strategy-consistent appraisals, and less individual gun-slinging that can undermine a vehicle's ROI potential. Second, the system gives appraisers latitude to make deals in the context of a dealer's appraising strategy objectives.

Give dealers the ability to evaluate appraiser performance in a more objective, meaningful, and strategy-minded way. When the dealer's automatically calling in the plays for every appraisal, performance measurement changes. It's no longer a subjective and often futile exercise to determine if appraisers are putting the right money on cars. Rather, the conversation becomes about whether they're executing the plays the dealer established, based on what the dealer strategically defines as the right money in any single appraiser situation.

Give dealers the ability to more closely manage appraiser performance. The system's appraisal strategy-setting and play-calling ability open a new door to measure appraiser performance. Dealers can assess how well appraisers heed the strategy-based plays, and coach individual appraisers to become more investment- and ROI-minded as they evaluate vehicles.

I am very proud of the appraisal system we developed for ProfitTime GPS. I believe we're bringing several "firsts" to the industry that elevate the art and science of appraising vehicles to a level that previously wasn't possible.

The next several chapters show you how the new appraisal system inside ProfitTime GPS can help you finally tame the Wild, Wild West that appraising represents today. The taming starts with you setting your appraisal strategy so the system can automatically call the right-money plays to your appraisers—like football coaches who call plays for their teams.

that, in fact, every vehicle's investment potential, or its profile of investment risk and opportunity, is unique. In turn, we recognized that the retail-based pricing strategy, which we helped bring to the industry, did not advance what should be every dealer's number-one objective in used vehicles—make more money or net profit in the used vehicle department. This backdrop leads us to the industry's third, next-generation used vehicle pricing strategy.

Third-Generation Pricing Strategy—Optimize Each Vehicle's ROI

This next-generation pricing strategy is built from the data science discovery that every vehicle has its own unique profile of risk and opportunity and, therefore, its own ROI potential. The data science work led to a pricing algorithm that's calibrated to price each vehicle in the live retail market to achieve its optimal ROI in an appropriate amount of time. The algorithm operates from a data-science-driven model that assesses the probability of any vehicle selling at any price in the next seven days.

Let me be clear: The algorithm isn't calibrated to price every vehicle to sell in seven days. That would be foolish, if not silly. Rather, it is applying its predictive pricing power to each vehicle's unique profile of risk and opportunity to determine data-science-driven retail pricing recommendations that will provide the highest statistical probability of any vehicle achieving its optimal ROI outcome in an appropriate amount of time.

The best practice for executing this ROI-minded pricing strategy is to price vehicles within the recommended ranges ProfitTime

GPS provides every day. The end result is the blend of patient, gross-minded pricing for your Platinum and Gold vehicle investments and more urgent, volume-minded pricing for your Silver and Bronze investments that I discuss in Chapter 6.

What does the ROI-minded pricing strategy look like in practice? It looks like the breakdown of Platinum, Gold, Silver, and Bronze vehicle investments in Table 13.1 (see Chapter 13). The respective days to sell for each precious metal category corresponds to its collective profile of risk and opportunity. Hence, when dealers follow ProfitTime GPS's pricing system recommendations, they will sell their Platinum and Gold vehicles in respective averages of 50 and 40 days, to optimize their high-gross ROI potential. On the other end, dealers will sell their Silver and Bronze vehicles at respective average days to sell of 30 and 20 days, which means they're selling more to drive volume because they're in greater investment distress.

When dealers achieve these optimal timeframes, they have eliminated the problem that plagues far too many dealers—they sell their Platinum and Gold vehicle investments twice as fast as they sell their Silver and Bronze vehicle investments. Or, to put it another way, they are taking twice as long to sell their worse vehicle investments than their best used vehicle investments. They are poster children for the inverted, irrational pricing profile I reveal in Chapter 6.

The data-science-driven, ROI-optimized pricing strategy that ProfitTime GPS supports also features an important philosophical foundation: That is, if you believe the best way to get into a vehicle is to know how to get out of it, then your pricing strategy must connect directly to your appraising strategy. ProfitTime GPS provides this strategic connection and, in another industry first for the system, makes it much easier for dealers and top managers to spot instances where the individual pricing your vehicles, unwittingly or willfully, breaks this investment- and ROI-critical connection, and you end up with the irrational, suboptimal pricing profile that too many dealers suffer from today.

Let's have a look at how this appraising-to-pricing strategy connection works to help you ensure the right money you establish in appraising never goes wrong when you price the vehicle.

CHAPTER 30

HOW PROFITTIME GPS CONNECTS YOUR APPRAISING AND PRICING STRATEGIES

Let's consider the two long-standing used vehicle inventory management principles I share in Chapter 29:

"You make your money when you buy the car."

"The best way to know how to get into a vehicle is to know how to get out of it."

None of us could say the principles are wrong. They are right as rain. They became foundational principles for used vehicle appraising and pricing because they're true.

But where the principles should meet—in exactly *how* you price your used vehicle investments—has been a persistent problem for most, if not all, dealers.

Think about all the times someone stepped up on a trade to make a deal and then priced the vehicle to make a big gross. How'd it go? I suspect the result was the same almost, if not every, time. The vehicle sat for too long, priced too high. When it finally sold, no one was happy with the outcome. And yet no one ever did anything to make sure it didn't happen again.

The problem in this situation, and so many others where, for whatever reason, the appraising-to-pricing strategy connection gets broken, is that no one has an appreciation for how the right money you establish in appraisals can go wrong as you price vehicles.

Here's what I mean: If you understand that you make your money when you buy the car, and the best way to buy the car is to know how you'll retail out of it, doesn't it make logical, sound sense to stay true to the strategy you used to acquire the car as you price it?

In the case of the trade-in you stepped up to acquire, the right thing to do, from an investment perspective, is to recognize right away that you stepped up, and you've created an investment-distressed asset—which should be priced to reflect the distress.

But that's not what happens. Why? Because there's never been an understanding of what the "right money" should be at the time of appraisal, and there's no recollection or recognition, when it's time to price a vehicle, of whether you brought the vehicle in for the right money or you didn't. In addition, as we discuss in a later chapter, there are often individual beliefs, biases, and financial interests that can cause the person pricing your vehicles to ignore or reject the strategy you used to appraise the car as they price it.

The vAuto team and I recognized that if we wanted to help dealers become more prudent managers of their used vehicle investments, and help them stop selling their best cars twice as fast as their worst cars, we needed to bridge this long-standing appraising-to-pricing strategy gap as we built the pricing system inside ProfitTime GPS. We also wanted the system to give dealers the ability to call the pricing plays, just as they now can in appraising, to minimize the influence of individuals who too often break the appraising-to-pricing strategy connection.

That's why the recommendations that the appraising system delivers to appraisers to acquire a vehicle, and those the pricing system provides to price the vehicle are, in fact, connected. Before I explain how the connection occurs, though, it's important to understand how and why they don't connect. The data science, and the algorithms that drive the appraising and pricing strategy-tied recommendations, are different.

For appraising, the appraisal strategy is driven by the algorithm that assesses each vehicle's investment value. The data science measures and weighs, in proper proportion, each vehicle's Cost to Market, Market Days Supply, and retail sales volume to determine its investment score on ProfitTime's 1–12 scale. As we discuss in the appraisal section, dealers establish their appraisal strategy by choosing the investment score that represents the right money for appraisals for their dealership, based on their preference to achieve gross, volume, or a balance of both.

For pricing, the pricing strategy inside ProfitTime GPS produces recommendations that are based in part on the investment score the dealer has established as their appraisal strategy target. But the primary inputs that drive the pricing system's ability to generate pricing recommendations for every vehicle come from three distinct places:

1. Everything we know about the vehicle in question. This data/information is largely derived from what the dealer tells the system about the vehicle through the appraisal process.

2. Everything we know about the current market and the vehicle in question. The system distills a host of factors on the vehicle and competing units from the live market data it constantly monitors.

3. Everything we know about the dealer's past experience and current inventory needs for the vehicle in question.

Even with this explanation, and the evidence that recommended pricing ranges vary from one vehicle to another, dealers think the recommended pricing ranges are simply tied to a specific investment score on ProfitTime GPS's 1–12 scale.

But that's not the case. For example, you can see these primary inputs at work through the way the system's recommended ranges land across the individual Platinum, Gold, Silver, and Bronze investment categories. The system doesn't always produce a recommended range that lands on the high side for a Platinum vehicle. The range could be positioned toward the middle or low end for a Platinum vehicle investment. Similarly, the system doesn't always produce a recommended range for a Bronze vehicle on the low side. If you've got a Bronze vehicle that works well for your store, the system will not produce a pricing range as if the vehicle's fully distressed.

Okay. That's how the data science and algorithms that drive the appraising and pricing strategies inside ProfitTime GPS are different and distinct. So how do they work together?

The connection point between appraising and pricing strategies in ProfitTime GPS starts with the way the pricing recommendations are calibrated, using the pricing algorithm and data science, to drive outcomes that tie to each vehicle's investment score. As explained previously, the pricing recommendations for a Platinum vehicle are calibrated so the vehicle can achieve its optimal ROI outcome in a more patient and appropriate amount of time. This outcome only occurs when the individual pricing your used vehicles follows the pricing system's recommendations for the Platinum vehicle investment from Day 1.

The same is true for a Bronze vehicle—the pricing recommendations will help you affect a faster, more urgent pace of retail sale to ensure the vehicle can achieve its optimal ROI. Here again, this outcome depends on the individual pricing your Bronze vehicle investment within the recommended range from Day 1.

The appraising-to-pricing strategy connection also extends to the appraisal itself. When an appraiser opens an appraisal, the recommended appraisal value range the system provides follows a "retail-back" assessment of the vehicle's investment potential, based on the investment score the dealer established as the right money target for their appraisal strategy.

Meanwhile, the pricing system uses the same "retail-back" assessment to produce recommended pricing ranges on the vehicle you've just appraised and acquired. To be clear, while the algorithms and data science that drive the appraising and pricing system recommendations mine the retail-back assessment of a vehicle for different purposes, each operates from the same live market view of the vehicle.

The end result of the connection points between ProfitTime GPS's appraising and pricing strategies and systems is that they work in harmony—attuned to each other to eliminate all the instances where the right money for a vehicle goes wrong when it's priced for retail sale. Or, to put it another way, the appraising/pricing connection in ProfitTime GPS helps reduce, if not eliminate, the instances where the person pricing a vehicle applies a different exit strategy than the one an appraiser used to value and acquire a vehicle.

I think most readers will agree their used vehicle departments would be better off if their appraising and pricing strategies remained more in tune and true to each other as they take in and retail their used vehicle investments. When this important connection occurs, the right money for any vehicle drives the right price that yields the most optimal ROI outcome.

But the pricing system inside ProfitTime GPS offers another benefit that, heretofore, wasn't available for dealers. In short, it shines light into the currently dark corners of used vehicle pricing that don't get noticed until it's too late to do anything about it.

Let's have a look.

CHAPTER 31

A SYSTEM BUILT TO FIX THREE USED VEHICLE PRICING PROBLEMS

Every dealer has felt an unfortunate end-of-the-month moment in used vehicles that goes like this: Your results are in for the month. You're looking at the used vehicle department's performance. You discover one of two unpleasant realities. Either you didn't do enough volume, or the department didn't generate enough gross.

The realization often triggers a conversation, where you and managers discuss what happened. Just as often, such conversations don't lead to much meaningful change or improvement. Sooner or later, the end of another month will arrive, and the realization that you didn't do enough volume or gross will manifest again.

The reality behind such month-end disappointments is that they often represent the collective result of a lot of distinct pricing decisions made by an individual, typically a used vehicle manager, that aren't connected to any broader strategy. Rather, they are driven by the pricing manager's biases and beliefs about each vehicle, its potential and/or the effect their decision might have on their paycheck.

The problem is, by the time we realize the collective results of the pricing decisions, it's often too late. The month's already finished. The results are already in.

When the vAuto development team and I set out to build the pricing system inside ProfitTime GPS, we were guided by two primary goals: First, we wanted a system that would elevate the art and science of used vehicle pricing by bringing the investment value potential of individual vehicles to the forefront. We wanted dealers and managers to know exactly where each car stood on Day 1 in terms of investment value and provide a path to pricing that would enable them to manage each vehicle to its optimal ROI potential.

Second, we want to reduce, if not eliminate, the frequency of the unpleasant, end-of-month realizations where it becomes painfully clear that the used vehicle department didn't do the volume or the gross the dealer expected or believed it would.

The development team and I spent a lot of time using the data science discoveries we'd made about used vehicle investment potential to study and understand what's really going on, month after month, as managers and others price used vehicles. Our research and study led to three important realizations.

The first thing we came to recognize is that the person who prices vehicles in the dealership is arguably the single-most important and influential individual who determines the monthly outcomes of the used vehicle department. We realized they essentially serve as the captain of the ship. Through their control of used vehicle pricing, the individuals have the wheel in their hands. They are steering the ship. As we analyzed the collective outcomes of their individual pricing decisions, we understood that sometimes the individuals steered the ship to a destination that wasn't necessarily intended or wanted.

The second thing we understood about the person who serves as the used vehicle captain is that each individual brings their own beliefs and biases to the job of pricing used vehicles. Based on our review of the collective outcome of individual pricing decisions, it's clear that each individual has a distinct approach to how they believe the job of pricing vehicles should be performed.

The third thing we realized is that the job of pricing used vehicles or steering the ship during a month, essentially occurs under the cover of darkness. By this I mean that, over the course of a month, the consequences of the many individual pricing decisions that occur aren't visible to anyone. To be sure, the consequences become very apparent and clear at the end of the month. But by then, it's too late to do anything about it.

With these foundational understandings, we set out to create a system that would shine light into the present state of used vehicle pricing darkness. We wanted the system to tie pricing decisions more directly to the dealer's overall investment strategy, which starts with each vehicle's appraisal. We also wanted to bring in-the-moment visibility to pricing decisions so they could be assessed and measured on an ongoing basis through the course of a month, thereby enabling dealers to determine the extent to which pricing decisions are consistent with their desired outcomes and strategy.

For example, as we talked about in the appraising section of the book, we know there are times when a dealer wants to go for gross, go for volume or strike a balance between both as they retail used vehicles every month. That's why we committed to building a pricing system that's calibrated to achieve the desired outcomes the dealer establishes through their appraisal strategy. In turn, managers who heed the pricing recommendations from Day 1 will more consistently price vehicles to achieve desired outcomes. We also wanted the system to give dealers and top managers a clear line of sight to know, at any point during a month, if their used vehicle ship is properly heading to their strategic destination of more gross, volume or a balance of both.

But most important, we also committed to building a system that, if dealers see that pricing decisions are not made in alignment with their desired outcome, they can be adjusted or course-corrected—so that dealers don't get to the end of month and face the unpleasant surprise of not achieving enough gross or volume.

Let's examine how this unprecedent, in-the-moment visibility into pricing decisions works.

CHAPTER 32

SHINING A LIGHT ON BELIEF AND BIAS IN USED VEHICLE PRICING

As I mention in Chapter 31, the individuals who make used vehicle pricing decisions in dealerships today have a lot of influence and power to shape the outcomes of the used vehicle department. They are, in effect, the used car captains who set the direction and course for the ship that represents your used vehicle department.

I also mention that the used car captains often make pricing decisions under the cover of darkness. It's true that some dealers might evaluate a used car captain's pricing decisions on current vehicles in inventory from time to time. But the reality is that pricing largely goes unnoticed until an unpleasant surprise occurs at the end of a month, and someone starts asking questions.

I would also add that the occasional reviews of a used car captain's pricing decisions are cursory or surface-level. The reviews might assess how a vehicle is currently priced in the market, but they most certainly do not get to the heart of the primary purpose of investment-minded used vehicle pricing. That is, if you believe that the best way to get into a vehicle is to know how to get out of a vehicle, then you should be pricing your used vehicle investments with same strategy you had in mind when you appraised and acquired the vehicle.

Historically, dealers haven't had the ability to see, let alone measure and manage, the degree to which pricing in their dealerships represent a proper extension of the dealer's established appraisal strategy, or a disconnect, where someone has broken this investment-critical connection, either unknowingly or willfully, as they price vehicles.

But that's exactly why the vAuto team and I developed the Pricing Alignment Tool inside ProfitTime GPS. The tool gives dealers the first-ever ability to see how well their appraising and pricing strategies connect, and to course-correct when there's clear evidence that this investment critical connection has been broken. In effect, ProfitTime GPS is helping shine a light into the dark corner of used vehicle pricing and, in doing so, is elevating the art and science of used vehicle pricing to a level that previously couldn't exist.

This chapter includes four examples of how the system's Pricing Alignment Tool gives you unprecedented, in-the-moment ability to see what's really going on with the pricing of your current used vehicles. It gives you an instant view of how frequently the connection between your appraising and pricing strategy is broken and a means to investigate the reasons why the break occurred. From there, you can course-correct, whether it means changing the prices on your current inventory to better reflect your appraisal strategy or revisiting your appraisal strategy itself.

Example 1: Rooftop A

In this dealership, the dealer's established an aggressive appraisal strategy to bring in vehicles and drive volume. The dealer cares about gross profit but it's a lesser objective compared to the goal of selling more vehicles. To achieve this goal, the dealer's established a target investment score of 3 in their appraisal strategy. The dealer's okay being aggressive to bring in vehicles at the high end of the Bronze investment category because they want to sell as many vehicles as they can in any given month.

As the dealer or top-level manager examines the Pricing Alignment Tool for this rooftop (Figure 32.1), they can immediately see that there are an awful lot of vehicles that are priced in a way that disconnects them from the dealer's aggressive, volume-oriented appraisal strategy. How can you tell?

Well, look at all the vehicles priced above the ranges ProfitTime GPS recommended to ensure each vehicle's pricing remains connected to the dealer's appraisal strategy. Across each investment category, you can see that the vast majority of times the used car captain at this dealership rejects the data science, they are pricing vehicles above the recommended range. Why? To go for gross,

ProfitTime Pricing Alignment

Metal	Recommendation Below	Recommendation Above	Aligned		
P	1	6	78%	⊘	⚠
G	0	5	69%	⊘	⚠
S	1	24	31%	⊘	⚠
B	0	48	19%	⊘	⚠
TOTAL	2	83	49%	⊘	⚠

Figure 32.1. ProfitTime pricing alignment for Rooftop A

which is a different objective than the dealer's aggressive, volume-oriented appraisal strategy.

Let's think about the consequences of these appraising-to-pricing strategy disconnects. The dealer's bringing in vehicles with a volume-minded appraisal strategy (a 3 on the ProfitTime investment scale). This objective means they've stepped up and put big money into vehicles, maybe too much money, and some vehicles in the current inventory likely already represent poor grosses or negative equity (i.e., the Silver and Bronze vehicles). And yet the used car captain has priced the vehicles to go for gross, which means they are likely priced not to move as quickly as they should.

To me, Rooftop A represents a used vehicle department where the pricing strategy, because of its disconnect with the appraisal strategy, is going to create suboptimal and unpleasant outcomes of aged inventory and low volume unless someone takes the time to understand exactly why the disconnections are occurring.

From my experience, there are two likely reasons for the disconnection between the appraising and pricing strategies at Rooftop A.

The first is that the used car captain is going rogue. For whatever reason, individual belief, bias, or self-interest, they have decided they need to make more gross for the used vehicle department. They are effectively ignoring the dealer's stated aggressive and volume-oriented appraisal strategy more often than heeding it. If nothing else, the dealer who sees this pricing alignment profile would be best served to start asking the used car captain some questions and potentially sitting them down to reprice some vehicles before the situation gets any worse.

But it might also not be the used car captain's fault. Another reason Rooftop A's pricing alignment shows such high numbers of vehicles priced for gross rather than volume could have come from the dealer. Maybe the dealer suffered a case of amnesia and forgot that they established an aggressive, volume-oriented appraisal strategy and, unhappy with the current state of used vehicle gross profit averages, told the used car captain to price vehicles to make gross.

Ultimately, it doesn't matter why the disconnections between the dealer's appraisal and pricing strategies are occurring. Rooftop A is headed for trouble, unless someone steps in and reprices the vehicles to reestablish the connection with the appraisal strategy, or the dealer decides their aggressive, volume-focused appraisal strategy needs to be changed.

Example 2: Rooftop B

Our situation at Rooftop B is almost the polar opposite of what we just reviewed with Rooftop A. At Rooftop B, the dealer's a gross-minded operator. They have established an appraisal strategy target investment score of 7, which means the dealer wants to be conservative and bring in vehicles as Gold investments, creating the opportunity for more retail sales with sizable gross profit potential.

But look at what's happening to the appraising-to-pricing strategy connection in the Pricing Alignment Tool example in Figure 32.2. In this case, the used car captain has priced an outsized share of the dealer's inventory below the ProfitTime GPS pricing recommendations, which are calibrated to achieve the dealer's conservative, gross-minded appraisal strategy objective.

When a used car captain prices vehicles below the recommendation, they are favoring volume over gross—which is not what the

ProfitTime Pricing Alignment

Metal	Recommendation Below	Above	Aligned
P	16	0	21%
G	22	2	38%
S	17	2	72%
B	9	1	63%
TOTAL	64	5	49%

Figure 32.2. ProfitTime pricing alignment for Rooftop B

dealer's appraisal strategy ordered. As a result, we now have a situation where the dealer is bringing in vehicles to drive gross, but the used car captain is pricing them to move quickly—cheap-selling the dealer's best Platinum and Gold investments while taking a serious haircut on the Silver and Bronze vehicle investments. The story here is that, unless someone does something to change course and realign the pricing to the dealer's conservative, gross-minded appraisal strategy, the used vehicle department will get to the end of the month where they sold a lot of vehicles but didn't make the gross profit they wanted.

Here again, the pricing pattern could be the result of the used car captain going rogue, opting for volume for some financial or personal reason. Or maybe the dealer forgot about their conservative, gross-minded appraisal strategy and ordered the emphasis on pricing vehicles to move quickly.

Either way, the outcome's still the same: The dealership is not going to achieve the gross profit objective they established in their more conservative appraisal strategy, and will leave money on the table as they cheap-sell their best investments. The current pricing strategy, if left unchanged, results in Rooftop B failing to capitalize on the opportunity they created when they appraised and acquired vehicles with the intention of making gross profit.

Example 3: Rooftop C

At this dealership, the worst of all worlds is happening in terms of used vehicle pricing. Rooftop C is suffering from a fairly sizable number of vehicles where the pricing is disconnected from the dealer's appraisal strategy, whether it called for being aggressive, conservative,

ProfitTime Pricing Alignment

Metal	Recommendation Below	Recommendation Above	Aligned
P	9	1	50%
G	11	3	41%
S	2	12	43%
B	4	32	45%
TOTAL	26	48	46%

Figure 32.3. ProfitTime pricing alignment for Rooftop C

or more balanced as they appraised vehicles. Unfortunately, the circumstances at Rooftop C are also the most common I see when I evaluate dealers' pricing alignment profiles.

In looking at Rooftop C's pricing alignment profile in Figure 32.3, it's clear to me that the used car captain at this dealership doesn't care that much for data science. More than half the time, 54 percent to be precise, this used car captain, who the dealer has trusted to make good decisions, is not a huge believer in data science.

But the pricing patterns, and the strategic disconnects they represent, should alarm any dealer. Why? Because the used car captain, beyond their unwillingness to trust data science, is most definitely going rogue, likely because of personal belief or bias, or for their own self-interest.

How can I say this? Well, let's look at the two clear patterns that emerge from the pricing alignment tool's window into the current state of Rooftop C's appraising-to-pricing strategy connection.

At first glance, you might think the pattern represents a used car captain who's all over the place, making random pricing decisions to drive gross and/or volume all across the inventory. This view, however, misses the darker nature of what's really happening.

The patterns here are anything but random. They are highly selective, representing conscious choices to go for gross on some vehicles and go for volume on others.

Look at the Silver and Bronze vehicles. When the used car captain says no to the data science on these vehicles, they price them almost uniformly above the recommended range in an effort to go for gross. Given that the Silver and Bronze vehicles represent investments with the greatest level of distress, the reality is that it's a fool's game to go for gross on these vehicles. They have the least favorable investment risk/opportunity profile. So why is the used car captain going for gross on these vehicles? To avoid the hurt and pain of pricing them within ProfitTime GPS pricing system's recommended ranges. Put another way, the used car captain doesn't want to face the reality that pricing the Silver and Bronze vehicles to move will be painful. But eventually they will need to be priced to move, and the only question that needs to be answered is whether it will hurt more to do it now or later. The answer is, obviously, that it will hurt much more later.

The end result: 50-plus percent of the dealership's used vehicle inventory is priced not to move, which will hurt the used vehicle department's ability to drive volume.

Now, let's look at the Platinum and Gold vehicles. See how they're almost uniformly priced below the recommended ranges? The captain's priced the inventory's best vehicles, the ones with the highest investment potential, below the recommended range to drive volume, effectively cheap-selling their best cars to compensate for the fact that they've priced more than half of the inventory, the Silver and Bronze vehicles, not to sell.

The used car captain's selective decision-making—which means they are cheap-selling their best investments and holding onto their worst investments too long—most assuredly does not represent the dealer's appraising or pricing strategy, whatever it may happen to be. The decisions reflect a desire to do what's best for the used car captain, not the dealer or the used vehicle department.

If I were the dealer, and I suspect the same is true for every dealer reading this book, it's simply not okay to drive volume by cheap-selling your Platinum and Gold investments just because you've overpriced your Silver and Bronze vehicles. From an investment and operational perspective, it's not okay for this used car captain to break the appraising-to-pricing strategy connection in such a self-serving manner.

Thankfully, with the pricing alignment tool in ProfitTime GPS, this dealer has the opportunity to set the used car captain on the proper course, or potentially find someone else to put the ship on course to a more ROI-favorable destination.

I would also add that the unfortunate circumstances occurring at Rooftop C strike me as the most discouraging. Why? Because they illustrate the persistent and pervasive nature of the traditional behaviors and beliefs that ultimately cause suboptimal outcomes for dealers. Dealers with used vehicle departments that resemble Rooftop C would be making more money and selling more cars if it wasn't for the behaviors and biases common among many used car captains.

Example 4: Rooftop D

I suspect the dealer at Rooftop D would be pleased as they look at their Pricing Alignment Tool in ProfitTime GPS (Figure 32.4). The dealer can see how their used car captain is handling used vehicle pricing, trusting the data science and staying true to their strategic appraisal objective to be aggressive to go for volume, conservative to go for gross, or to go for a more balanced blend of volume and gross.

The dealer's first observation might be that the used car captain has learned to trust data science, while still relying on their experience and judgment to make the call on some cars.

You can see the used car captain accepts ProfitTime GPS pricing recommendations 85 percent of the time. I appreciate any time I see a used car captain accepting 70 percent to 85 percent of the

ProfitTime Pricing Alignment

Metal	Recommendation Below	Recommendation Above	Aligned
P	4	1	89%
G	1	2	90%
S	2	3	83%
B	2	5	82%
TOTAL	9	11	85%

Figure 32.4. ProfitTime pricing alignment for Rooftop D

recommendations because it tells me that while they trust data science, they recognize when it might not be telling them the whole story about a vehicle.

To be sure, there are legitimate reasons why the pricing system inside ProfitTime GPS might produce a recommended range that a used car captain might question. The system can't see the vehicle's color, condition, or any aftermarket products that might affect the vehicle's appeal in the market.

But the used car captain can see such things and, in this example, the captain has decided to overrule the pricing recommendations. I'm willing to trust that this used car captain is making good decisions when I assess how they price vehicles when they reject the recommendations.

Do you see a pattern? Neither do I. The fact is, this used car captain isn't following their bias or belief when they decide to reject a recommendation. There doesn't appear to be any willful decisions to avoid the hurt of a troubled investment or failure to demonstrate the proper patience on a high-ROI vehicle.

When the used car captain at Rooftop D says no to data science, they price some vehicles above the recommendations, and some below the recommendations. It's fair to presume that this disparate treatment reflects a used car captain doing their best to price each vehicle the way it should be, while heeding the dealer's strategic objective, whether it's to go for gross, volume, or strike a balance between both.

Based on my experience working with dealers, I'm well aware that the conditions reflected in Rooftops A, B, and C are happening in dealerships across the country every single day. The problem is that dealers don't have the ability to see it, much less do something about it.

But that's exactly the problem we worked to solve as we built the pricing system inside ProfitTime GPS. For the first time ever, dealers can see what's really going on with their used vehicle pricing and how often it departs from their strategic appraising and investment objectives. The pricing system also gives them the ability to adjust course with their used car captains whenever it's necessary to meet their objectives and before it's too late.

To be sure, the visibility and accountability that ProfitTime GPS brings to the current dark corner of used vehicle pricing isn't easy for some dealers or used car captains to accept. After all, pricing has occurred in the dark for so long. The level of accountability and oversight ProfitTime GPS provides is unprecedented and likely to make some uncomfortable.

But, as outlined in earlier chapters, if dealers want to thrive in used vehicles in the months and years ahead, they will need to find a way to at least set aside their discomfort and distrust. Instead, they should apply themselves to harnessing the power of data-science-aided decision-making that ProfitTime GPS provides to help them become the more prudent managers of their used vehicle investments that today's used vehicle business requires.

PART VII

THE ELEPHANT IN THE ROOM

CHAPTER 33

WHY WE NEED SCIENCE, STRATEGY, AND SYSTEMS MANAGEMENT—*NOW*

Let's take a moment to revisit and reflect on an important reality of today's car business I share in Chapter 1.

I outline how we've reached a turning point in used vehicle profitability. I make the case that the return on investment (ROI) in used vehicles has been on the decline for the past decade or so because of the ever-rising investment costs of used vehicles and the static or declining front-end grosses that have occurred as a result of the ever-growing efficiency of the wholesale and retail used vehicle markets. I call the circumstances a "turning point" for our industry because they represent a fundamental shift in every dealer's ability to make money as they retail used vehicles.

I go even further here. I'd call the ongoing decline of used vehicle ROI as one of the larger elephants in the room for dealers. It's a situation no one really wants to think about or discuss, especially when, for all intents and purposes, the actual economic and financial pain of the circumstances isn't being fully felt, noticed, or understood by dealers.

But there's no mistaking that the ROI in the used car business is eroding. I don't think anyone can make the case that the used vehicle profitability or ROI erosion will stop. At best, it might decelerate. At worst, the pace of decline will increase.

What to do? It seems to me that we need to acknowledge the elephant and face the reality of what lies ahead. From where I sit, it seems certain that every dealer will, at some time, need to operate differently if they hope to achieve ongoing growth, success, and sustainability in their used vehicle departments. We all must face the fact that as our investment costs in used vehicles go up and our gross profits diminish, the success of our used vehicle departments will be in jeopardy if we stay the current course.

I'm not suggesting that dealers won't be able to make money as the ROI erosion progresses. Despite the margin and ROI pressure, I believe there will always be "juice" in the car business. The difference today, however, is that current methods of used vehicle management are not engineered to help dealers extract the juice they need or want from used vehicles as ROI erosion advances.

But that's exactly what the combined power of the superior data science, the ROI-minded Variable Management strategy and the ProfitTime GPS system that supports the management strategy bring to the table for dealers. If the end goal of any dealer is to extract the optimal amount of ROI juice from every vehicle, then you need a blend of science, strategy, and system management that recognizes each vehicle has its own unique profile of investment risk and opportunity and helps you manage it accordingly.

I realize my embrace of the elephant in the room and its ROI implications for dealers might strike some readers as dark and dour. But I believe our current moment—and the current opportunity the moment presents—require the clearest view of where the used vehicle business is heading.

On a more positive note, however, I also don't think the road ahead for dealers will be significantly more challenging than the last time market conditions called for a fundamental rewrite and revision of the used vehicle management playbook. That transition began as the internet became more than just a place where a few tech-minded individuals gathered to connect, ping a search engine for information, or share music.

Despite the cries that the internet would kill the car business, it didn't. It simply changed the nature of how the car business worked. As your frontline and showroom moved online, dealers adapted as fast as they believed they should, with some moving much faster than others. We all made investments in technology, people, and training. We reshaped our used vehicle management strategies and our processes to thrive in what had become an internet-driven business.

In other words, dealers rose to the occasion. They took advantage of the science, strategy, and systems management that was available at the time to help them make the necessary transition to operating their used vehicle departments differently.

That's exactly where we stand today. If the ROI juice is slowly getting squeezed out of the used car business, dealers must find new ways to capture a larger share of the juice that still exists. In my view, that's where the data science, the investment-minded Variable Management strategy and the ProfitTime GPS systems management that supports it enter the picture.

But let me be clear: You can't just buy the system we've built and expect the data science and strategy to guide decision-making. You'll need to get your team on board with the principles of the new, ROI-minded used vehicle playbook. To be sure, vAuto Performance Managers will be by your side to help, but the responsibility of changing how you do business will rest on individual dealers.

From working with dealers who've made the transition to the data science, the ROI-minded Variable Management and the ProfitTime GPS systems management that supports the strategy, there are a few critical change-management must-dos:

- Everyone needs to know the "why" behind your decision to lean into the science, strategy, and systems that will help you optimize each used vehicle's ROI potential.
- Everyone needs to know your strategy and its objectives.
- Everyone needs to know how to use the system to help them execute the strategy and achieve its objectives.
- Everyone needs to know you'll be holding them accountable to your defined strategy.

- Everyone needs to know the performance metrics you'll be using to judge their competence, talent, and compensation.

You can bet that achieving each one of these "everyone needs to know" outcomes will take some work. Dealers may have to dig deep to muster the leadership and change management skill they'll be required to exercise as they commit to an ROI-minded approach to managing their used vehicle investments.

But as noted previously, dealers have a track record of rising to the occasion.

Perhaps one way I can help everyone rise to the occasion is to offer some key performance indicators (KPIs) that, based on my experience working with dealers who've become prudent, ROI-wise used vehicle investment managers who understand the proper blend of science, strategy, and systems management, suggest you're headed for the improved ROI outcomes you'll need to achieve to secure your future success.

Let's have a look.

CHAPTER 34

TOP-LINE, SYSTEMS-MANAGEMENT-DRIVEN KPIS FOR YOUR BIG THREE

I've always liked a line that John Malishenko, former chief operating officer for the Germain Motor Company in Ohio, used as he talked about dealership management priorities: "You have to manage and measure the inputs to get the outputs you expect."

There are variations of the principles behind this statement that are likely familiar to many readers. "You must inspect what you expect." Or "If you're not measuring, there's no way you can properly manage."

As the vAuto team and I developed the science, strategy, and systems management that Variable Management and ProfitTime GPS offer to dealers, we understood that the only way dealers might successfully transition to a new, ROI-minded approach to managing their used vehicle investments would be to ensure that our system provides dealers and top managers with key performance indicators (KPIs) to help them measure and manage the effectiveness of their strategy and its execution across their Big Three of vehicle acquisition, appraising, and pricing.

The KPIs associated with the ROI-minded Variable Management strategy are different than the metrics dealers have traditionally used to oversee their used vehicle departments.

With an investment-minded strategy in place, it's no longer enough to talk about how many units you sold, the grosses you averaged, or the age of your inventory in management meetings. To be sure, those things still matter.

But now we must orient the meetings around the KPIs that help you manage your team and inform whether the inputs they create are leading to the outputs your ROI-minded used vehicle investment strategy requires.

The good news is that dealers have been here before.

Let's remember that prior to the rise of the internet, dealers and managers had no concept of the mission-critical metrics that became the norm as the second generation of the used vehicle playbook came into existence. Market Days Supply. Price to Market. Cost to Market. vRank.

vAuto introduced these management metrics and they became the mission-critical measurements dealers used to manage their used vehicle performance and results—and assess the ability and skill of their key players to achieve the outcomes the dealer expected.

The new KPIs provide a means to measure and manage the effectiveness of your ROI-minded used vehicle investment strategy and the effectiveness of your team's execution of the strategy across the Big Three. Here's a sampling of top-line KPIs for vehicle acquisition, appraising, and pricing.

Vehicle Acquisition

As discussed in Chapter 19, the principal objective of any dealer's vehicle acquisition strategy should be to optimize the inventory portfolio so that it consistently reflects the right number and mix of vehicles to meet the dealer's investment strategy objectives and the demand/supply dynamics in a local market. To that end, it'll be important for dealers to mind at least the top-line KPIs that can indicate when the right number and mix of vehicles in your inventory investment portfolio is on target or trending off your target objective.

Right number of vehicles: ProfitTime GPS allows you to see at a glance how the number of vehicles in your current inventory compares to your rolling 30-day total of retail sales. The ultimate goal is to consistently maintain a 30-day supply of vehicles for optimal investment management efficiency. Our experience working with ROI-minded dealers who follow the Variable Management strategy reflects the fact that this KPI can fluctuate but that you should not see your days supply dip to 20 days or balloon to 40 days for any extended period of time.

Right mix of vehicles: The critical KPI here is your Inventory Mix Index, which reveals how closely your current inventory mix matches the strategic objectives you established. The index also tells you how well your current mix compares to what's selling in your market. This metric is essential to understand whether your vehicle acquisition strategy and related processes are producing an investment-optimized inventory portfolio.

Appraising

As discussed in the appraising chapters (Chapters 21–28), it's now possible for dealers to establish what they believe the "right money" should be for every vehicle they appraise and acquire. The right money is defined by each dealer's appraisal strategy and the investment value target it specifies for individual vehicles. ProfitTime GPS provides two top-line metrics to help dealers measure and manage the extent to which individual appraisers are heeding the strategy and the right money as they appraise vehicles, and whether the appraisal strategy itself might need an adjustment.

Target appraisal score: Since this KPI establishes the right money for every vehicle you appraise, it's important for dealers to revisit their target appraisal score to make sure it's consistent with current market conditions and their investment objectives, which can change. Generally speaking, we see ROI-minded dealers at least review, if not adjust, their target appraisal score once a month.

Percentage of appraisals on strategy: This KPI is very straightforward. It gives you an overall view of the share of the appraisals your appraiser team completed to acquire inventory that fall within the recommended ranges (or plays) the appraisal system inside ProfitTime GPS calls in for individual appraisers and vehicles. Our experience with ROI-minded dealers suggests that this metric should show roughly 80 percent of appraisals landing on strategy, a figure that accounts for the instances when going off strategy is the right thing to do. I would also add that you'll likely see some variance in the metric when you evaluate it across sourcing channels. For example, while you'd ideally want your percentage of on-strategy appraisals to be consistent across all channels, the realities of appraising vehicles in the showroom versus an auction, for example, are different. The end goal is to use this metric to determine each channel's sweet spot and manage to it.

Pricing

As we discuss in the pricing chapters (Chapters 29–32), the ROI-minded Variable Management strategy falls apart if you do not price your used vehicle investments with the same exit strategy you used to appraise and acquire them. Similarly, the Variable Management strategy works best when you price vehicles according to the recommendations ProfitTime GPS provides from Day 1 to achieve the variable turn policy that ensures your Platinum, Gold, Silver, and Bronze vehicle investments sell in an appropriate amount of time.

ProfitTime pricing alignment percentage: You can understand this KPI at any time by reviewing the Pricing Alignment Tool inside ProfitTime GPS. It shows you how well your vehicle prices in your Platinum, Gold, Silver, and Bronze investment categories align to the system's pricing recommendations. Generally speaking, we see top-performing ROI-minded dealers maintain a roughly 80 percent alignment, a figure that allows for managers to price above or below alignment when they determine the specific characteristics of a vehicle suggest the vehicle's pricing should fall outside the recommended range. The Pricing Alignment Tool is also a critically useful feature in ProfitTime GPS's pricing system to help you spot the pricing behaviors of individual managers that reveal when their bias or belief results in vehicles priced out of alignment with your strategy.

Average days to sale by investment category: As I outline in Chapter 13, when ROI-minded dealers are pricing their vehicles in accordance with the pricing recommendations ProfitTime GPS provides from Day 1, you should see a waterfall-like effect in the days to sell for each vehicle investment category. Generally speaking, we see top-performing ROI-minded dealers move their Platinum vehicles in an average of 50 days; Gold in an average of 40 days; Silver in an average of 30 days; and Bronze in an average of 20 days. The averages may vary some for individual dealers but the end goal is to be more patient with your best vehicle investments (i.e., Platinum) and more aggressive and urgent with your worst vehicle investments (i.e., Bronze).

When dealers mind and manage these top-line KPIs and use them to guide individual performance, we generally see them achieve the optimal outcomes we'd expect from a well-executed ROI-minded Variable Management strategy—your gross *and* your volume improves as you and your team work in concert to optimize the ROI for each used vehicle.

It is my sincere hope that this rundown of KPIs gives you a baseline understanding of how you'll need to conduct your management meetings to build the trust, buy-in and improved performance of your teams to help you effectively and fully adopt the ROI-minded

Variable Management strategy and the ProfitTime GPS systems management that supports it.

I'm 100 percent certain that dealers who embrace the KPIs and the ROI-minded Variable Management strategy they help you execute through your teams will be the ones walking past the elephant in the room that's keeping everyone else in a corner.

EPILOGUE

A FUTURE VIEW OF SCIENCE, STRATEGY, AND SYSTEM MANAGEMENT

One of the central tenets of the ROI-minded Variable Management strategy is that each used vehicle has its own unique profile of risk and opportunity. As I've tried to lay out in this book, our new understanding about the unique nature of each used vehicle upturns a host of traditional management practices that weren't really pointed toward the outcome of optimizing each used vehicle's ROI potential.

As the vAuto team and I developed the ProfitTime GPS system to support the ROI-minded Variable Management strategy, we began to ask an important question: Is there any aspect of variable operations in a dealership that wouldn't benefit from connecting to the same strategic idea that you should aim to optimize the ROI for every asset in your new and used vehicle portfolios?

Our answer? No, there isn't. This realization led us to think about how the principles of Variable Management might extend to every new and used vehicle, and how we might give dealers the ability to exercise an ROI-minded strategy across all aspects of new and used vehicle inventory management.

New vehicles: To be sure, dealers have arguably more control over their new vehicle investment portfolios than they did in years past. Still, there's far less room for dealer discretion in shaping the ideal investment portfolio in new vehicles compared to used vehicles.

But shouldn't that be the end goal of original equipment manufacturers (OEMs) and dealers? I'm 100 percent confident that as data science advances, we'll soon have the ability to predict, perhaps down to colors and trim lines, the equivalent of Platinum, Gold, Silver, and Bronze vehicle investments in dealers' new vehicle inventory portfolios. I have no doubt this day will come, and I can tell you vAuto's data science team is already headed in this direction.

To be sure, cracking the code of new vehicle investment value will be far more difficult than used vehicles. From a data science perspective, the way OEMs turn incentives on and off across their product lines adds multiple layers of complexity. It makes creating, testing and proving algorithms that correlate the probability of a vehicle's sale to its price extremely difficult. Or maybe it won't be so difficult as OEMs move to offering more vehicle identification number (VIN)–specific incentives.

I don't know. But what I do know is that as ROI pressures grow in new vehicles, you can bet the data science will point to better ways of retaining and optimizing each vehicle's ROI, whether it's great, good, bad, or ugly.

Merchandising: Some dealers use generative artificial intelligence (AI) tools like ChatGPT to generate descriptions for online used vehicle listings. Others have rules-based tools that automatically adjust the placement or ranking of new and used vehicle listings to improve their visibility in filter/search results on classified sites.

However, the real end game with merchandising any new or used vehicle is to do so in a way that has the highest probability of connecting that vehicle with the specific buyer(s) looking to purchase it, while optimizing the ROI of your merchandising spend on the vehicle itself. This sort of thing happens with online advertising all the time.

But online vehicle listings aren't yet as dynamic and targeted as they will be in the future—an opportunity that data science will inevitably inform, if not create.

Reconditioning: A long-standing challenge here is that dealers often don't really know what's happening with reconditioning. Why? Well, as we talk about in Chapters 21, 25, and 28, the uncertainty starts with reconditioning estimates in your appraisals. From there, it's another dark corner of the dealership.

Too often, no one knows what's happening, with any specific vehicle, or what's being (or has been) spent. That's why dealers who, at a minimum, start tracking their reconditioning performance find they spend less and get cars through the shop faster.

But can we envision a day when each used vehicle gets a data-science-driven, ROI-optimized recommendation for how much *should* be spent on a specific vehicle? You can bet that day is coming, too. The current disconnects and unknowns in reconditioning represent a loose nut data science can most certainly tighten.

F&I: Speaking of dark corners in a dealership, I'd submit that, in many dealerships, the F&I manager decides what kind of F&I opportunities each vehicle, and each customer, represents—even if they're supposed to be following a standard, menu-based presentation. But what might a data-science-enabled assessment of the vehicle, along with the customer's long-term ROI potential for the dealership, suggest? The answer's unknown today, though I suspect it's only a matter of time before we find out.

The key purpose of this chapter is to get everyone thinking about how the combination of ROI-minded data science, strategy, and systems management that is now available in used vehicles eventually can, will, and should elevate all aspects of variable operations in a dealership.

We're not there yet, but I don't think anyone can argue that we'll know someday soon what a data-science and ROI-optimized dealership looks like and how it should operate. The evolution's already underway, and it'll only gain momentum as more dealers realize how critical maximizing the investment value and ROI of every new and used vehicle will be for their dealership's future profitability and success.

ACKNOWLEDGMENTS

I must share a little-known fact related to the books I've published over the years. You see, I'm not a writer who locks himself in a room with a computer or typewriter and, after many hours, days, and weeks, emerges with a book in hand.

Instead, I spend countless hours deep in thought about what a book might say, and then I get help to translate the concepts and messages I've developed into written form. Since my first Velocity book, the person I've leaned on to help me translate my ideas and thinking into manuscripts has been Lance Helgeson, a former industry reporter and writer I first met almost 20 years ago, when he did a story about my first company, mPower Auto. For this book, I've given Lance proper due as a coauthor in recognition of his dedication and hard work for many years as my right hand for writing.

This book also would not be possible without the contributions of a host of other individuals at Cox Automotive. The list is too long to run down here. These individuals know who they are.

But, closer to home, there is absolutely no way I'd have anything to say, in book, blog, or other form, without the privilege of working with Chris Stutsman. He's a bright, brilliant person who, over the years, has helped me harness the power of data, data science, and sound, strategic thinking to push the boundaries of the technology and tools our industry uses to manage used vehicle investments.

I also must acknowledge the ever-present hand of my assistant, Susan Taft. Beyond the fact that she helps me get where I need to be and connected with who I need to talk to, Susan serves as our sharp-eyed proofreader to make sure the book reads the way it should.

Closest to home, I hold a profound sense of gratitude and love for my wife, Nancy, our three sons and their growing families. Nancy gives me room to roam with my work and writing. She's the glue that keeps our family close and committed to each other. It's a special gift that affirms the saying that behind every great man there's a great woman.

Finally, it's important to acknowledge you, the reader, for your interest in this book and my perspective. It's my sincere hope that this book feeds your thirst for new knowledge and new ways to run your business better.

ABOUT THE AUTHORS

DALE POLLAK began his retail automotive career nearly five decades ago, when he sold vehicles at the age of sixteen at his family's dealership in northwest Indiana. In 1985, he became a Cadillac dealer in Elmhurst, Illinois. His interest in used vehicles and technology led to the launch of vAuto and the pioneering Velocity Method of Management. Since joining Cox Automotive in 2010, Pollak has led efforts to drive integration-minded innovation across the company's auction, media, and software divisions. As a retail automotive thought leader, Pollak has written seven books, speaks frequently at industry events, and has served as an NADA Academy instructor for the past fourteen years. Pollak received the 2010 Ernst and Young Entrepreneur of the Year award, entered the Chicago Area Entrepreneurship Hall of Fame in 2014, and now serves as a transportation advisor to the Federal Reserve Bank of Chicago. Pollak earned a bachelor of science degree in business administration from Indiana University, earned a law degree from DePaul University's College of Law, and is a four-time winner of the American Jurisprudence Award. Pollak and his wife, Nancy, live in Austin, Texas, where they enjoy spending time with their three sons and their growing families.

LANCE HELGESON serves as director of industry analysis for vAuto. In this role, Helgeson helps shape vAuto's messaging, marketing, and thought leadership efforts on behalf of the company and founder Dale Pollak. Before joining vAuto, Helgeson served in editorial and leadership roles for newspapers and business-to-business publishers, including *Dealer Magazine* and *Car Dealer Insider*, as well as online public relations and reputation management agencies. Helgeson graduated with honors from the University of Maryland, College Park, earning a bachelor of science degree in journalism. Outside of work, Helgeson plays drums with Chicago-area bands, most notably the Hoyle Brothers. Helgeson lives in Oak Park, Illinois, with his wife, Nina, and their two children.